Lillian E Curtis

Patchwork: Juvenile Poems

Real, Incidental and Imaginary

Lillian E Curtis

Patchwork: Juvenile Poems
Real, Incidental and Imaginary

ISBN/EAN: 9783744713566

Printed in Europe, USA, Canada, Australia, Japan

Cover: Foto ©Thomas Meinert / pixelio.de

More available books at **www.hansebooks.com**

Patch Work:

JUVENILE POEMS.

Real, Incidental and Imaginary.

By LILLIAN E. CURTIS,

AUTHOR OF " FORGET-ME-NOT."

Timidly, little work, I launch thee on the vast literary sea;
   But though vividly thy shortcomings may appear,
   May'st thou find some to hold thee dear—
To look kindly on thy imperfections, and place thee in their affections.
   May'st thou be the germ to future blossoms, rich and fair,
Blossoms that may redeem features where thou dost fail;
   And may you, readers, who peruse this bud with care,
Pause lightly where you find its interest pale;
   And, lenient reader, may you your kind attention loan,
   Give it a place within your heart—a place within your home.

CHICAGO, ILLINOIS,
1875.

NOTE BY THE AUTHOR.

DEAR READERS:—Some of you are already acquainted with
my writings through the medium of "Forget-me-not"—that book
of childish rhymes which, in fancy, at least, paved the way to a
castle of literary hopes for the future. Yes, my first and scarcely presentable effort, you, generous and considerate reader, gave
a warm and welcome reception, even beyond my most sanguine
expectations; and as a reward for your patience and lenity over
a child's scribbling, I purposed to offer as a successor to that
crude attempt, "The Casket," a volume of about four hundred
pages, on which I had been engaged since the publication of Forget-me-not in 1872; but finding myself totally debarred of that
pleasure, I make the best of a bad matter, by asking your attention to a patched-up substitute, viz.: "Patchwork:" so called—
but I will leave the origin of the title to your imagination, which
undoubtedly it can supply without difficulty. Suffice to say that
the fire of July 14 was the cause of the MSS.' destruction, and
also of a large canvassing list for the same. This modest volume,
then, which *chances* to make its debut before you, may you, gentle
reader, look upon kindly and without repulsion, considering if
that fatal fire had not occurred, the unassuming petitioner would
not have been asking for a share of your attention; but, alas, on
just such slender threads hang even the greatest of life's events.

L. E. C.

CHICAGO, Nov. 18, 1874.

DEDICATION SONNET.

FRIEND of my infancy, still friend of my youth
    Friend whose love hath ever been mine,
Friend of virtue, valor, wisdom and truth,
    What a life of lovely devotion is thine :
Thy feet uncomplainingly tread the rough paths of duty,
    And thy service welling up from love's purest store,
Bubbling out with graceful, angelic beauty,
    O'er thy darling's head doth constantly pour :
Thine assistance, advice and counsel in this world of strife
    Were richer than a crown in rubies set,
O'er the sky of my young and inexperienced life,
    And thy guidance and teachings may I not forget :
Kind teachings that my faltering steps direct,
    And urge within right's castle railings,
That coming years (if seen) a life may yet perfect,
    Which hath now so many failings :
Ah, loving arms that fondly, affectionately extend,
    To bring me within a pure life fold,
Know, I count thee my most precious friend,
    And my wealth of gratitude is untold,
And as a token of these professed and ardent vows—
As my scattered rythmic waifs I house
    Within the embrace of this unpretending book.
Though in it no Shakesperian *brilliants* shine,
    Kindly upon it thou wilt look,
Because they're thoughts and sentiments of mine ;
    Accept, sweet mother, friend considerate and kind,
Whose affection floweth unaffected nor stilly,
    This simple wreath that for thy brow is twined,
    By thine own affectionate Lilly.

WABASH AVENUE, CHICAGO, Oct. 29, 1874.

PATCHWORK--JUVENILE POEMS.

LEND A HAND.

What is this world?   A playhouse that God for man hath built,
  And some by fortune are favored more than others;
Then, favored ones, upon this platform of woe, and want, and guilt,
  Oh, assist your struggling, wayside brothers!
      You, who on fortune's eminence chance to stand,
      Ope the heart and lend a hand.

Pity those who drink from Adversity's bittered cup,
  Who trials and troubles count by the score,
Oh, help to lift sad, despairing ones up,
  And God and man shall bless your store!
      And seeing one on the margin of despondency stand,
      Ope the heart and lend a hand.

To-day Fortune may smile —to-morrow, may frown,
  To-day we may be hugged in Prosperity's arms;
Such is life! while some go up, others come down
  Into the midst of Misfortune's alarms,
      Hence, if high on the ladder of fortune you stand,
      Ope the heart and lend a hand.

Then, in this wilderness of contention and strife,
  Life, for all, might become a bright dream,
By assisting those whose trials and struggles are rife,
  Those pulling hard 'gainst Adversity's stream,
    For those combating rough winds on life's changeful strand,
    Ope the heart and lend a hand.

HOPE.

Hope! Star to brighten the darkest day;
To guide us e'er o'er life's rough way;
To aid us up the steepest, stoniest hills;
To cheer the heart that sorrow fills;
To dispel the clouds so black and dense;
To quiet anxieties deep, intense;
To comfort the heart with a hidden care;
To relieve the captives of dark despair;
Then, beauteous, golden Star,   .
With a radiant light that shineth afar,
Still, when eyes shall close on earth's misty vision
Be our support to life's bright Elysium.

A FRIEND.

'Tis well to feel there's one somewhere,
  As with life's struggles we contend,
Who can our joys and sorrows share,
  Whom we may call a friend.

Eagerly we ope the message white,
    That its way to us doth wend,
And read, with hearts so gay, so light,
    The signature of a friend.

What joy the fact when it cometh first,
    What rapture doth it lend,
When the truth upon us burst,
    That we've a new-found friend.

WALKING IN THE SNOW.

Up and down through the busy street,
We hear the tread of tramping feet,
Back and forth we hear them go,
Crash, crash, through the frozen snow.

Sad or merry the reverberating sound,
Of the tread, tread, o'er the frozen ground;
As it carries one back to the long-ago,
Back, at the sound of the creaking snow.

Sad memories to some perchance it brings back,
From the golden depths of a by-gone track,
Recalling hopes that in ashes lie low,
Castles built in the crashing snow,

That may have fallen to dust on the ground
Hence, it may seem a mournful sound ;
It recalls the loved of the long-ago,
Who walked with us in the beautiful snow.

The stars glimmer dimly over our head,
While feet keep up their ceaseless tread,
And the heavens with frosty sparkles glow,
Over the crash of the pearly snow.

But sad or merry the reverberating sound,
Of tread, tread, o'er the frozen ground,
It carries one back to the long-ago,
Back, at the sound of the crashing snow.

LUCY'S SUMMER SEASON.

June's glorious sun was pouring down
   His fiercest, blazing rays,
When Lucy left the bustling town,
   To spend the Summer days;
And a crowd gathered at the close of day,
   (For she was daughter of a millionaire,)
To bid farewell, as the Night Express bore away
   The heiress rich and fair,
And she took each proffered hand,
   But not a tear she shed,
For they eyed the mansion grand,
   O'er poor Lucy's head ·

No conscience was for *any* pleading,
   She thought no *one* the best ;
And while from her native home receding,
   She pictured the fair West.

Breezy lake and fairy isle were left behind,
   Hills, mountains, vales passed by,
Bright fancies sat in Lucy's mind,.
   Yet she did not repress a sigh ;
When five days and nights had fled,
   And she neared her journey's end,
Feelings of loneliness were not dead,
   She wished she had a friend ;
But Lucy was unwavering, and not afraid
   To carry bravely through
The firm, well-founded plans she'd laid,
   To gain a love, unfading, true ;
Aside were lain both friz and curl,
   And every pretense of fashion,
And Lucy was a table-girl,
   In Col. Graham's mansion.

The August sun had sunken in the west,
   The breeze blew calm o'er lawn and lea,
When little Lucy, weary for want of rest,
   Sought her seat by the garden tree.
" Must I to happiness bid farewell ?
   Ah, yes, for I've carried the ruse too far,
I can't revoke it now and tell,
   And surely he'll love none but Fashion's star."

" Lucy," 'twas Clifton Graham's voice,
  " Please not be angry if I come,
Nor—if I love you, my heart's own choice,
  Don't tell me you are poor, loved one."
The happy wife smiles as home friends tease,
  And conjecture more or less,
She thinks, let them imagine what they please,
  The secret they'll never guess.

THINK OF ME.

TO ANNA C————, BOSTON.

WHEN round thee is lingering nothing but joy,
No vexation or aught to annoy,
Only gentle gales sweep o'er life's lea,
          Oh, then think of me !

When life to thee is so exquisitely gay,
And joys come with each new-born day,
Howe'er excessive thy pleasure may be,
          Oh, then think of me !

When friends and fortune are smiling,
And amusement thy leisure time is beguiling,
While only the blue of Fate's sky you see,
          Oh, then think of me !

Though the deep gulf of miles loom high between,
Before you an eastern, before me a western, scene,
Ah, walk sometimes by the beach methinks I see,
    And there think of me!

But when the hurricanes of life are dashing around,
And hail-storms of strife fall thick on the ground,
When looking out on Adversity's vast sea,
    Oh, then think of me!

When storms of sorrow o'er thee are sailing,
And brightest of joys before thee are paling,
When friendships are fast receding from thee,
    Oh, then think of me!

Where'er thy step in the future may glide,
Whether on land or on ocean tide,
Whether joys or sorrows dwell with thee,
    Oh, think sometimes of me!

Think of me as one who will ever befriend,
And the warm hand of friendship ever will lend,
Whenever the smile of a friend you would see,
    Oh, then think of me!

ONE HAD A FORTUNE, THE OTHER HAD NONE.

GEN. L. was a peculiar man, and owned a fortune immense
    He had his whims, alike he had wealth,
Hence, he counted his outgoings by shillings and pence,
    Deeming economy, perhaps, conducive to health;
But while the shining god is hugged by the old,
    It seldom lingers in young people's sight,
And thus his two sons, and his heap of gold,
    Perplexed him morning and night.

But the youngest ran away and went to college,
    Thereby incurring the old man's displeasure;
The other staid home and dispensed with knowledge,
    And thus gained the coveted treasure.
The old man died, the attorney dwelt on his will, at length
    It showed the rash, unwise act he had done,
In his fading health, and failing strength,
    For he'd left one a fortune, the other had none.

The easy won fortune went on the swiftest of wings,
    And he's a poor, ignorant man to-day;
The other has a hard earned fortune that clings,
    It came not in a hurry, nor hurries away.
A fortune were well, if managed with prudence and care,
    But if winds of Adversity o'er you are blown,
Remember, e'er you sink down in despair,
    One had a fortune, the other had none.

ATLANTA.

ATLANTA ! fair city of the sunny South !
Here, within thy outstretched arms,
I've spent a few brief hours,
True, some clouds have marred the charms,
Within thy golden bowers;
Yet, when I hang the picture on Memory's wall,
I'll choose the brightest side of all.

Atlanta ! fair city of the sunny South !
Shadows, and not all smiles,
We meet on life's boisterous tide,
And out of the dark and cloudy defiles,
Should we single the Golden Side ?
Thy beauties of merit I would not deny,
And *that* picture shall hang before my eye.

Atlanta ! fair city of the sunny South !
I this hasty, poetic tribute bring to-day,
And kindly offer thee,
And should Fate waft me again this way,
Wilt thou remember me ?
Banish the clouds, and let the sunshine dwell,
Atlanta ! as I whisper thee farewell !

TO MY FORMER TEACHER.

My Teacher! instructress true of former days-
Remembrance, in a thousand ways,
    Enfolds thee in her arms;
And here in this delightful Southern bower,
Memory, at this twilight hour,
    Recalls thy mind's rare charms.

And from her castle fancies rally,
To picture a spot of Oriskany's fair valley,
    A sunny, sloping, little glen,
Where the gentle zephyr breathes,
And Beauty spreads her choice wreaths,
    Ah, dear old Cottage Sem!

With many a weary mile between,
Many a valley and mountain scene,
    Mid the Southern moonlight beauty,
Remembrance, faithful to her trust,
Tramples Forgetfulness in the dust,
    And stands at her post of duty.

Among the pictures on Memory's wall,
O'er which the curtain of Time doth fall,
    There's one fair little gem,
That brings many a hidden thought to light,
And many a by-gone scene to sight,
    Ah, dear old Cottage Sem!

Many a month has passed away,
And many a fair and cloudy day,
    Since I left my Northern soil,
Yet, o'er this golden crested clime,
Where the birds all winter chime,
    Must Friendship's tendrils coil.

Still how oft Memory speedeth back,
To touch on that familiar track,
    That fair and shaded glen,
Whether sunshines or clouds are overhead,
Fancy her brilliant wings doth spread,
    O'er yonder Cottage Sem !

PRESS ON !

INSCRIBED TO C. C., BOSTON.

PRESS on ! press on ! though trials assail,
Countenance never a word like fail,
Press on ! press on ! with courage three-fold,
When Fortune frowns and Fate looks cold,
Though darkness appears to obscure all the light,
Look straight toward the temples of Truth and Right ;
Press on ! with firm will and motives true,
For there's many a prayer ascends for you ;
Press on ! with a will totally undaunted,
The prize you seek shall sometime be granted ;

Press on! most noble, self-sacrificing soul,
You shall surely win that coveted goal ;
Press on! press on! nor let anything daunt,
Not the scornful laugh, nor the jeer, nor the taunt,
Be inspired! for round that heavenly seat
Hath been said shall the " pure in heart " together meet.

Press on! mid Prosperity's smile or Adversity's fall,
Remembering there's One who careth for all,
One who our footsteps ever will guide,
Then press on, and turn not aside;
Storms may rise, temptations come fiercer and stronger,
Press on! press on! enduring yet longer.
Words of cruel contempt and malignant scorn
May deftly o'er your innocent head be borne,
From lips that no divine praises share,
Lips that discard sacred words of prayer,
Still, press on! to Distrust a total stranger,
He will lead you past every danger;
Press on! press on! at whatever cost,
Your patience and labor shall not be lost,
You shall meet your reward, if faithful you've stood,
When the Saviour pronounces, he " hath done what he could."

WE DIE TOGETHER.

A GALLANT ship sped o'er the deep blue sea,
   Swept along by the swift, smooth tide,
And the happiest one that sailed in her glee,
   Was a young and lovely bride;
And he who had nobly won her heart and hand
Was bearing her to his own native land.

And ever and anon she looked with laughing eyes
   Into that smiling, attractive face,
Wishing for famed Italy's sunny skies,
   His native soil, his birth-place.
Onward, onward, the noble vessel fleetly sped,
While joy in their hearts illumination shed.

The stars shone with a brilliancy to inspire,
   And all were securely locked in slumber,
When the knell like cry of fire! fire!
   Startled the sleeping number;
Hoarse shouts rose 'mid the sickening gloom,
The watery waves must be their doom!

But no! a manly spirit the sailors cherish,
   Though hands with blood be laved,
The women shall not be let to perish,
   But they can *alone* be saved.
Husbands, fathers, in the flames must die,
And they bid the weeping ones good-bye.

"Quick!" the captain says, with extended hands,
  And beckons to the youthful bride:
But undaunted and firm she stands
  By her valiant husband's side.
" Nothing our hands of love shall sever,
  If die we *must*, we'll die together."

The ship went down beneath the billowy wave,
  Perished in the volume of fiery flames,
And 'mong those who found an ocean grave
  Were those two world-bright names.
May those sweet words float on, on forever,
"If die we *must*, we'll die together."

THE FLOWER GIFT.

MID the future years that come and go,
  The fair or clouded hours,
Memory oft her doors ajar shall throw,
  To admit these beauteous flowers:
Gratitude doth her fairest hand uplift,
To thank you for this floral gift.

ANDERSON, S. C., April 18, 1874

/

THE HEART'S OWN STORY.

A GAY, joyous laugh and a bright, winning smile,
  A countenance beaming with mirth,
And the motley world is opining the while :
  " He's the happiest being on earth."
They see his fair fame, with fortune he's blest,
But ah, the heart knoweth its own story best !

The laugh may be forced, the smile be assumed,
  The mirth, a mask of deepest disguise,
And dark wells of sorrow are often illumed,
  By an artful dissembling of eyes ;
And the world fancies Joy where Despair is a guest,
For ah, the heart knoweth its own story best !

On a wintry day when the sun shines bright,
  We think, what delightful weather !
And wonder people are bundled so tight,
  And pulling their mufflers together ;
But we feel not the cold that's piercing their breast
For ah, the heart knoweth its own story best !

The smile-wreathed face is oftimes the saddest,
  Gay corsage may flaunt o'er a bleeding heart,
The brain with grief is oftimes the maddest,
  As it some sparkling witticism impart ;
No one may judge by the fairest test,
For ah, the heart knoweth its own story best !

ON VISITING MT. AUBURN CEMETERY.

WE step beneath the iron archway overhead,
And enter the silent city of the dead
Here, stretching out before the eye,
More than a hundred acres lie ;
Forming a home for those once gay,
Whose prosperous lives have passed away.
Up Central Avenue, pausing by a statued grave,
Then on to the chapel erected for the brave,
Casting on this a greeting and farewell,
Thro' Ivy and Geranium paths, on to Hazel Dell ;
Here a bubbling fountain by night and day
Tosses its wreaths of foam-white spray,
Its silvery particles into a misty vapor rise,
Like a gorgeous bridal veil before the eyes.
But we leave it playing in its mystic power,
And, passing on, behold the lofty tower,
And climbing to the observatory looming high,
Distant landscapes can we descry—
But hark ! like a solemn, deep toned knell,
Falls the stroke of the warning bell.*

BOSTON, 4 P. M., Sept. 17, 1873.

---

* At 4 P. M. the bell in the tower strikes to warn visitors to leave the enclo-
sures.

A MOTHER IN HEAVEN.

OH! who wittingly can wander from the narrow way?
Who can perversely go toward Ruin's brink so gray,
Base passions, impure precepts, to obey;
    Who has in Heaven a mother?

Oh! who can willfully drink the cup of sin,
Strive Earth's empty bubbles to catch, to win,
Form a character transparent, dark, and thin,
    Who has in Heaven a mother?

Ah! who can deliberately walk on Satan's brink,
And calmly of his impious poison drink?
Who can rush on, nor stop to think,
    Who has in Heaven a mother?

NOT TOTALLY LOST.

Response to a poem entitled " Am I Totally Lost?"

THO' from the beaten path, perchance, you have strayed,
And pictures with dark spots in Memory are laid,
    Pictures that truth and honor have cost,
Turn back, nor think you *must* meet a deplorable end,
As a matter of course, for there's still time to mend,
    And you are not totally lost.

Do friends spurn you and contumely pass by,
Does there seem no pardon from even on High;
    If in shipwrecks of doubt you are tost,
The past missteps may not be obliterated, 'tis true,
But redeemed with regrets, and pure aims in view,
    For you are not totally lost.

Sink not in despair, let not hope nor courage forsake
There are few in life who make no mistake,
    Some less temptations accost;
Despair only need come when remedies are ended,
Never for fractures that still may be mended,
    And you are not totally lost.

If rash acts have made you outcast and forlorn,
The evening is dark, and darker the morn,
    Showers of acrimony o'er you are tost;
All need a draught from the sin-forgiving-cup,
Instead of sinking lower, strive to rise up,
    For you are not totally lost.

ACROSTIC.

Ever within my heart, sweet, precious Mother,
Lieth one surging thought, above all other,
Its spontaneous gushing thou need'st not doubt,
Zechin could never, ah, never, drive it out;
Around each tendril its clinging fibres clasp,
Bound firmly, as with an iron grasp,
Ever, *more firmly*, shall they twine,
There, sweet Mother, shall they shine,
Here let me say *that thought* is thine.

Care, born of misfortune, its way may wend,
Under it all behold in me a friend;
Rough brambles may our pathway fill,
'Twill but inspire one who loves you still,
In every vicissitude believe me dutiful,
Sweet Mamma, staunch friend and truthful.

CHICAGO, Nov. 3, 1874.

A BRIDE TO HER HUSBAND.

WRITTEN FOR MISS MARY B———.

Now, confidingly I place my hand in thine,
  (May it be a helping hand,)
  And pledge myself by thee to stand,
Whether clouds are dark or the sun does shine;
So thou art e'er unfaltering true to me,
Fidelity's hand shall ne'er be withdrawn from thee.

My cup of joy seems full to overflowing,
  Yet may I see sorrow and tears,
  But alike in all the coming years,
In love and patience will I be growing;
Of this I dream while standing by thy protecting side,
To welcome joy and love, who crown me as a bride.

I feel the pressure of thy encircling arm,
  May that same, through the tempests of life,
  When storms of adversity are rife,
Be a shield mid fierce peril's alarm;
Trials can I bear for they e'er must accrue,
But woe to thee, if thou shouldst e'er prove untrue.

Love's links are closely bound together,
  So securely they might last for aye,
  But should the cement prove nought but clay,
They'd break, and, breaking, break forever!
By faith and education I stand your equal,
We may be happy—time must tell the sequel.

From no olden ties have I to part,
  For no one living, or in the grave sleeping,
  Ever held a place within the heart,
Which now I place in thy keeping;
And still I'll not exact as much from thee,
Be it but a *whole* heart thou giv'st to me.

But time will change the face now fair,
  And she who stands where praises glide
  To crown the head of a youthful bride,
Will a look of wan dejection wear;
And furrows will sit on this unwrinkled brow,
Say, wilt thou love me then as now?

True, no dark forebodings by doubt are pressed,
  There's no feeling not joyous and free,
  Of perfect love and trust in thee,
There's no lurking twinges of unrest,
For guardian spirits that round us be,
Seem whispering " your bridal sure is blest."

Yet time works changes we little reck,
  Circumstances make a friend a foe;
  Lay our highest hopes in ashes low;
Destroy the castles that Faith may deck;
Still, Faith sails on reliant golden wings,
And Truth and Honor can do great things.

In the light of God our voyage we'll begin together,
  May He lead us o'er life's surging tide
  Thus may we cross to the other side,
Having known Distrust's dark cloud, ah, never,
And wake to know that, tho' we have failed,
Our sacred vows have not been assailed.

TO AN OLD SHOE.

I WAS having a regular rummaging to-day,
And there I found it stowed away,
    And brought it from its corner;
Ah, yes! shoe, though worn and old,
Once to feet merry and slightly bold,
    You served as an adorner.

Well, part of you is gone, 'tis true,
And she is gone who wore you;
    But I'm going to stand you there,
And gaze upon you as I choose—
No, but you needn't now refuse,
    Because you look not fair.

The day was bright and Nature smiled,
When I stood with her, the darling child,
    Near the spot I found you;
She shook her tresses of bronzy gold,
Her foot peeped from the merino's fold
    Then, you were new, old shoe.

What a lovely pair of shoes, I said,
And absently she bowed her head,
    Crowned with its golden glory;
How happy, Leilia, you must be, said I;
And then she drew a long, deep sigh,
    The signal of a story.

But why repeat the story of those lips?
Too well 'tis known that Wealth oft sits
　　With scepter that naught but frowns dispatch;
She smiled on Love, tho' it was poor,
And forbade to enter the carvéd door,
　　Wealth with Poverty could not match.

Rapidly my heart began to flutter,
Not a word my feeble tongue could utter,
　　As a drop of healing water;
That she so sad a story should tell,
Who was both beauty and belle,
　　A millionaire's only daughter.

Love conquered that time—ah, well!
But 'tis the saddest of sad, sad stories to tell,
　　For elopements bring little but woe;
They would go o'er the water; her father sometime—
Ah! would repent—it sunk, the White Star line,
　　And a curtain o'er the scene we throw.

I'll endite a rhyme—the simplest thing—
Just to tell what sorrow elopements bring,
　　Though Love be ever so true;
That you may accomplish some good to-day,
Ere I lay you forever away,
　　Away with the past, old shoe.

LINES TO MY MUSIC TEACHER.

With gaze u꠰ on the future's paths, mystic and uncertain,
   I turn one thought adown the vista of the past,
And Memory lifts her fair, informal curtain,
   With radiant raptures all o'ercast,
For she toucheth on many a scene in her sacred bower,
And combines them all in this parting hour.

The cheerful conversation and favorite book's kind loan,
   The deftly copied music in my hand,
What for these memories can e'er atone,
   Though on endearing spots I stand ?
And wait, there's still something I would not retrench,
While we cannot speak, we yet may write in French.

Each fond scene, as from day day to day we've met,
   Is woven with ties Friendship engraves,
And Memory her brightest star hath set,
   Where their united banner waves ;
What charms association benignly lends,
We met as strangers—we part as friends.

The lessons of the term they all are past,
   And we meet with saddened heart,
And though with joy, still with regrets o'ercast,
   For we meet, alas, to part ;
And we know, peering toward Uncertainty's mystic shore,
As teacher and pupil, we may meet no more.

Together we've gleaned instruction for the mind,
   And many an invention planned,
And links were formed that our heart-strings bind,
   While the depths of investigation we planned :
Recollections that Memory e'er must cherish,
That her warm clasp will ne'er let perish.

In all the future hours, oh, forget me not,
   Still hold my memory dear,
For tho' roaming o'er a distant and charméd spot,
   In imagination, I shall meet you here ;
'Tis courage now that I strive to muster,
As I leave the spot round which fond associations cluster.

And Conscience opes her magic eyes awide,
   And bids me thank you, o'er and o'er,
For modest Patience's perpetual glide
   From her purest, choicest store ;
While music itself was to you a treat,
I fretted o'er each new turned sheet.

And when the heart would its troubles borrow,
   You spoke words of comfort still,
Pointed me to the bright to-morrow,
   Through Hope's gentle rill ;
By your sympathetic words, and smile as bright as sun,
The heart's pure offering you have won.

Looking out on the boundless ocean of life,
   Where constantly before the eye,
Joyous pantomine scenes of the past are rife,

Lips decline to say good-bye;
Though friends I find worthy of my selection,
Keep me, I ask, e'er in your affection.

The heart feels what lips refuse to speak,
    Unspoken volumes hath the eye,
The tongue itself is childish, weak,
    For it trembles o'er good-bye;
If on earth we chance no more to meet,
May we walk one day Jerusalem's golden street.

We part, but though wide apart our paths are lain,
    We'll still be one in aim and in desire,
The link of friendship binds, a Saviour holds the chain,
    He holds the harp, the well-tuned lyre;
We part with swelling heart and tear dimmed eye,
But God is smiling o'er this good-bye!

Accept my gratitude and adieus, though unspoken,
    Anticipate what faltering lips deny,
Which means, linked with Friendship's fairest token,
    My teacher, friend, good-bye!
And when life, with its vicissitudes, is o'er,
May we meet again where parting is no more.

FRIENDSHIP.

FRIENDSHIP! how boundless and expansive is the term,
Leading thro' labyrinths—ah! 'tis a priceless germ.

Friendship! ah, it may look from many a smiling eye,
When bright life's sunshine and clear the sky.

But when the storms of adversity round us are pressed,
Then is the time for friendship's true test.

When the dark waves of trouble are surging around,
Then may the rare gem of friendship be found.

One by one the false gildings will all fall away,
While the pure and unfading jewel alone will stay.

The genuine gem of friendship how little we know,
Till the fierce winds of trial and misfortune blow.

If found by the stranger afar from lov'd native soil,
O'er fond Memory's bower should its tendrils coil.

WILMINGTON, N. C.

A SCENE FROM THE WINDOW.

A RARE and laudable incident hath just met mine eye,
    Would that such, though trifling, were not so rare,
Were they not, bluer far would be life's sky,
    And its labyrinthine paths more fair :
A humane kindness or trifling courtesy that all *might* show,
From the highest of life's walks to the lowest of the low.

If the latter, excuses should partially exempt;
    The former, what plea shall we present for them
Who ostentatiously, with lofty air, attempt
    The current of worldly wrongs to stem?
But in unstudied kindness, void of outward guise,
An inborn grace, a natural loveliness, lies.

The rain was drizzling slowly, and Nature wore a frown,
    A little lad moved aimlessly along the vacant street,
A wagon, rolling swiftly out of town,
    The little fellow joyfully ran to meet,
And ask the sun-brown driver for a bit of ride;
Kindly he stopped, and placed him at his side.

There was no repulsion to wound his tender heart,
    No angry gesture and sour look;
Would the world at large such kindly acts impart,
    Easier were read the pages of life's complicated book.
And will not each trifle be entered on those pages,
To be undimmed throughout the endless ages?

LINES TO LITTLE LEONARD.

THE vesper hour of service o'er,
You clasp my hand at the Chapel door,
Child of Innocence's purest store,
   How warm a clasp and true !
The tempests that o'er my life have blown,
Have ne'er round you been thrown,
For 'tis petty trials, I'm sure, alone,
   That have dared to stare at you.

And I know, whate'er the world may say,
That loving hand will ne'er betray
The one that leads it o'er the way;
   And nothing, I know, will change
The childish thoughts which you express,
The truthful words which you confess,
The innocent love which you profess,
   Nor e'er our hearts estrange.

A child, and therefore'll prove true,
Through the closest test, the strictest view,
I e'er might dare to look to you
   For friendship of the heart;
And tho' but confessions of a child,
Gentle, loving, pure and mild,
Better than professions excited, wild,
   And by a trifle rent apart.

OVER THE SEA.

WRITTEN FOR MISS S————.

My heart is restful, and I long to go far out, and over the sea, you
  know,
To go, to go, is all I care, for, ah, my true love dwelleth there ;
Summer's just shedding a parting tear, beck'ning Autumn to draw
  near,
And ere she steppeth from the strand, I may view Italy's sunny
  land,
And I may turn my eyes on the beauties of France's golden
  skies,
But, oh, may I gaze, above the rest, on fair Germany as the best,
For wasn't the darling of my affection born within her warm
  protection?
As on that far-famed soil I stand, may I learn to love that win-
  ning land :
Thoughts rush together, and all agree, to light on *one* far o'er the
  sea.

WHEN I WAS NELLIE LANE.

My heart was light from morn till night,
  Ne'er a thought of care had I,
Fair was the cloudiest day, and every month a May,
  E'en bleak December's sigh.

Ah, shall I tell it you ?   I had a lover true,
  But he owned no costly mansion ;
There, for Nellie Lane, must be a wide domain,
  Grand and broad in its expansion :
So Lord Delney asked my hand, and calmly I did stand,
  And sell my heart for gold ;
Oft, with anxious pain, I wish myself Nellie Lane,
  With bitterness quite untold.

SERENITY.

BE not with grief or joy o'ercome,
  'Tis a transient thing at best ;
Not till this life's work is done,
  Shall we find enduring rest.

PLYMOUTH ROCK.

WITH reverent step I approach the old historic rock
  On which, one day, in years gone by,
The Mayflower band, the Pilgrim flock,
  Sat with a weary, downcast eye,
And thoughts, in a chaos, running o'er and o'er,
For they were on a strange, a foreign shore.

Then, in that distant, but to them decisive, hour,
    They stepped on this teeming land,
Their ship the first, the old Mayflower,
    That touched this fruitful strand ;
They stood on an unexplored but verdant soil,
With hands for labor and for toil.

Carver, with his many a fair and wavy lock,
    And Standish, with such powerful zest,
Sat them down on this seashore rock,
    Awhile to plan and rest;
While Somerset, the Indian Chief, advanced—half bent,—
To see the angels from heaven sent!

Cautiously and with scrutiny he advances,
    To gaze on the strange, wild scene,
Penetrating are the swift and many glances,
    While his searching eyes with wonder gleam ;
He little knew, standing with gestured hand,
How soon the dark race must leave their native land!

O'er the rock, round which they met that day,
    A canopy now is looming high,
And the wild, dark race has been swept away,
    As an act of the long gone-by;
Yet there remains a portion of the old, mystic rock,
Where rested the Mayflower band, the Pilgrim flock.

PLYMOUTH, MASS., August, 1873.

LINES TO FRIENDS.

My visit is o'er, still Memory one lingering glance awaken,
  Mingled with a coterie of joyous thought,
O'er the various walks and rides we've taken,
  And the happy hours they've brought;
Aud if I have urged you from your way,
  Or taxed your patience sore,
Remember, and trouble me some day,
  Full as much, or more;
This visit's scenes fond thoughts must cluster round,
And e'er with fair memorial wreaths be crown'd.

One last fond glance around the hill-side spot,
  Wreathed with gems from Nature's dell,
Methinks the breezes sigh, we'll forget you not,
  As I whisper them farewell;
And around this beauteous landscape fair,
  Fondest memories will ever cling,
The Mohawk's murmur through the air
  That reached me in the swing.
Ere I come again, how many seasons shall cycle round,
Or shall I ever step on this delightful ground?

Truant Memory threads the mazes of the past,
  The time when I was here before;
She pauses beside a grave, at last,
  With grass and hedges growing o'er:

And there, weaving golden links, she's busy;
  Though no stone bears the name,
She knows the sleeper there was Lizzie,*
  Unknown in streets of Fortune, or road to Fame.
" Come and see me," was mingled with her last good-bye,
  I've been to see thee, Lizzie, where thou lie.

O'er the picture, an artist's brush would fail:
  The tones of the Sabbath bell upon my ear,
Above, the tiniest cloud's white sail,
  The Weeping Willow drooping near;
A scene worthy of deep thanksgiving;
  I sat beside her lowly bed,
And heard the voices of the living,
  While I mingled with the dead.
So mysterious our fleeting, uncertain breath,
We, too, should be prepared for death.

Swiftly circles Time's wierd, eventful tide,
  By mansion, grand, and cottage, plain,
And to the bright home upon the hill-side,
  May come changes of joy or pain;
But list! through rippling breezes of the air,
  Oft when the day is done,
The lingering accents of a prayer,
  My friends, for you will come;
And Fancy, I oft shall wing her hither,
  To see if one memorial bough shalt wither.

---

* Lizzie was a lovely young woman who sometimes made it her home with my friends.

And Imagination, ah, yes, shall oft meander
　Back to these endearing haunts,
To picture you o'er the fuchsia and oleander,
　And other cherished plants;
But oftener, o'er childhood's human flower,
　Watching its progress from day to day,
Pointing it toward yon heavenly bower,
　O'er the straight and narrow way.
Good-bye, and believe that my purest wishes lie,
Interwoven with that word, good-bye!

MEETINGS AND PARTINGS.

In the dèpôt, or the railway car, perchance,
　Or mayhap in the crowded street,
'Tis like a rare poem, or a thrilling romance,
　Thousands as strangers meet :
An hour, a week, a month flits by,
　And round each pulsing heart
Friendship has bonnd a golden tie,
　When they are called, alas, to part.
Yes, they who unfamiliar strangers met
　Are called to part in tears,
While Memory has her signet set,
　To shine in future years.

Little know we, standing on Uncertainty's threshold vast,
   Whom we may meet to love, part with to meet no more,
As turning an eye down the vestibule of the past,
   We launch our barque on Fate's mystic shore.
Methinks that the saddest of life's sad, sad things
   Is to meet to love, and when a brief space is o'er,
And limited hours have fled on arrowy wings,
   To part, to meet on earth no more! no more!
Friends, near and dear to us as our own connection,
   We tearfully press to our throbbing heart,
Sadly twine o'er them the wreath of fond affection,
   For we have met, alas, to part!

   But such is this changeful world of ours,
      That bitter close to sweet must cling,
   As December's snows and May's warm showers
      The varied seasons bring;
   And in this world, spacious and so wide,
      Some firm, staunch friends we find,
   But are hurried swiftly along the tide,
      To leave them soon behind.
   Yet oft we weave ties not easily broken,
      Though sundered for aye apart,
   And we cherish each word and token,
      They've won a place within the heart;
   And when o'er life's last refulgent ray,
      May we meet around that Throne,
   Meet to spend a long, perennial day,
      Meet where parting is unknown.

IN MEMORY OF FRANK CURRIER.

INSCRIBED TO MRS. CURRIER, BOSTON.

THOUGH there's a vacant place in thy household now,
And a look of sadness sits on thy brow,
And each day drags and is hard to measure,
Since parting with thy favorite and earthly treasure.
While thou unconsoled still weepeth for him,
Jesus hath welcomed the lost, loved one in.
From this world so cruel, bitter and cold,
Hath brought him into the Shepherd's fold.

Free from treacherous life's fierce alarms,
Think of him safe in the Savior's arms,
While wan grief haunts your once quiet pillow,
He knoweth sin nor sorrow's surging billow;
When you have passed life's turbulent helms,
He awaits you in those radiant realms;
In that peaceful land all free from care,
Father, mother, brother, sister, he awaits you there.

Called in the spring-time, the morning of life,
To step from the waves of trouble and strife,
Where no more he shall hear sin's dark waters roar,
To rest for aye on a brighter shore;

Pain cometh not there, nor grief's bitter tear,
Blest thy lost one, loved and so dear;
The May-day life that bid so brightly to bloom
Shall blossom more brightly beyond the tomb.

Gone in the innocent morning of youth,
Bearing the shield of purity and truth;
Gone from life's steep hills and bramble-filled track,
And would you to-day wish him back?
Though he has left your fond, loving side,
'Tis but to cross the bright, silvery tide;
And in that world where all is so fair,
Dear friends, know, he awaits you there.

PARTING LINES.

WE met, floating on life's e'er changeful tide,
 We met and some bright moments spent together;
When lo! the step of Parting glideth to our side,
 And our paths diverge, perhaps, forever!

Fickle and unstable is the barque of life,
 Round which fierce and stormy billows rage,
But while wrestling with the waves of strife,
 Will there e'er rest our memory's page.

Will e'er rest there at morn or twilight hour,
 The name of her you knew so short a time?
And will e'er a finger from friendship's bower,
 Point towards a form like mine?

Fateful and mystical are our varied days,
　Interspersed with many a weird, fantastic scene,
And oft we meet events on our destined ways,
　That seem like some vague dream.

But let me ask this much of you,
　Be our meeting recalled in a similar light,
When sometimes it shall rise to view,
　Oh, may *that dream* be bright!

Oh! please to count the moments all together,
　Henceforth an oasis of the Past;
And though the hand of Parting now sever,
　May their memory always last.

Here 'mid the perfume of blooming flowers,
　Beneath this genial and sunny clime,
Within these inviting Southern bowers,
　We met, we part for time.

Let one sad tho't with this parting moment blend,
　Though seasons come and go,
Remember, this is the hour, my friend,
　We part, to meet no more below.

Though this city you may not admire,
　Still that on memory's sheet
You'll place one spot is my desire:
　'Tis Second and Market street.

And should you, in future years, pass by,
  With friends so prized and dear,
Turn thither to this spot an eye,
  Dimmed by a falling tear.

And when back to your Northern home you go,
  Back to your native landscapes fair,
Let Memory wide her bright arms throw,
  Me in their embrace to bear.

My friend, I wish for you that Joy may prove
  Abundant in her blessings rare,
That she may give you happiness and love,
  Unmixed with toil and care.

Or if that could not be and she should send
  Trials and privations unto you,
May kind Providence a heavenly influence lend,
  To waft you bravely, nobly through.

A silent handclasp, and all is o'er,
  Henceforth, apart we'll dwell,
Just as we part to meet no more,
  Accept my final, yea, last farewell.

WILMINGTON, N. C., Feb., 1874.

SILVER WEDDING VERSES.

oys almost unclouded seem showered from above,
　While a Century strikes her quarter hour,
'o recall that moment when young and trusting Love,
　Opened the door of his fair, celestial bower,
ind bade up his beauteous isle, with sacred anthems, glide,
i true, devoted lover, a fair and youthful bride ;
ind the days that have so swiftly and so gayly flown away,
　Show that Love's bright bower has been kept with care,
'hat the light of each other's life has gilded each new-born day,
　And naught but mutual harmony has been permitted there ;
'he sympathy and kindly counsel ready e'er to lend,
iuffice domestic wants minus assistance of a " Mutual Friend."

i Century strikes her quarter hour to memorize that day,
　When, with stars of Faith o'erhead, up affection's blissful isle
'ou passed, with hearts their trust should ne'er betray,
　And vows issued from lips wreathed with a smile ;
Vell might those now in life's morn lift a grateful voice up,　.
ind try to glean an extract from the wine of such a pure life-cup.
Tis inspiring just as a cloud to-day hangs o'er the world,
　And we're tempted to doubt if there's a love that never dies,
io these precious leaves from a true life volume we unfold,
　And feast once more our hungry eyes :
fust in time with its soothing elements of harmony all fraught,
fust as we felt this world were dwindling down to naught.

Once more we're brought back by Reality's sonorous voice,
　　To know there *are* those, though far and wide apart,
Who, when they give their hand to the object of their choice,
　　Heaven be praised! they likewise give their heart;
Oh, that we could far more frequent scan the instance o'er,
Where yes once said, remaineth *yes* forevermore.
Twenty-five years of happiness, we may not say unclouded,
　　For life, for all, hath its dark hours ever,
But if shadows have at times your lives enshrouded,
　　How bravely, truly, were they shared together,
Thus lifting together burdens of foul anxiety and care,
Making life's pathway not of thorns, but roses fair.

And now we would ask that o'er these lives so blest,
　　The angel of Peace may henceforth hover,
That no feelings of uneasiness, or shadow of unrest,
　　E'er lurk beneath her fair wing's cover.
Twenty-five years of mutual enjoyment spent,
We predict the coming ones filled with calm content;
May welcome blessings e'er be shed,
　　And never round you be known to slumber,
May silver turn gold around your head,　　·
　　And diamonds join the number.
That this slight memorial tribute one happy moment lend,
Is the sincere wish of one you may deem a friend.

CHICAGO, August 31, 1874.

THE MARBLE HEART.

(INCIDENTAL POEM.)

THEY pass me by with a smile and a bow,
   And linger with low-spoken words by my side,
They twine wreaths of affection over my brow,
   And all possess love, fortune and pride.

But the trammeled heart beats not at their coming,
   And notes not their glances or tone,
Heart that would fain towards the lovelight be running,
   With a music to equal their own.

For all of them wonder, nor dream of the ashes
   Buried from the world's eyes apart;
And not dreaming of a sorrow that clashes,
   They term it a marble heart.

But they pass from sight, all these loves of mine,
   And the heart heedeth not their sigh,
But clings to a love that was wont to shine,
   One time in the long gone by.

Heart that hath beaten for *one*, from all others apart,
   Will cannot recall a flutter that's o'er,
Call it, if they will, then, a marble heart,
   For 'twill never know love any more.

GALENA.

FLOSSY and light was her hair, and her face was fair,
   Her form genteel, and her manners gay,
But one April day cool, a messenger entered our school,
   And bore our pet classmate away.

FIRE.

OH, demon, with thy scorching breath and fiery hand!
   And thou hast let thy venom and fury rest
Once more upon this fair Western land,
   Nor spared the Queen City of the Imperial West!

Once more Chicago has beheld her dark-wreathed foe!
   And once more has bent beneath his withering blast;
Again felt the heavy and unlooked for blow,
   With its direful clouds so thickly overcast!

But though thou hast trampled treasures to us so dear,
   Memorial gems, valued next to our own life,
It shows us we should have no idols here,
   In this transient battle-field of toil and strife!

Though thy forked tongues did lap mercilessly around us,
  Laying a lifetime's hopes low down in the dust,
After the first wild grief's o'er, we interpret thus,
  Not in earth, but in Heaven, should be our trust!

CHICAGO, July 14, 1874.

OCTOBER.

JOYOUS, sunny days, so bright and clear,
  But, oh, how short a time they last!
For ere we dream their close is near,
  Summer has joined the past:
While we rush on, nor dream that summer's done,
We're greeted by the rays of autumnal sun.
Swiftly the days have glided by,
  That have passed beyond recalling,
Withered and blighted the flowrets lie,
  The autumn leaves are falling;
And over many a gorgeous Nature-painted scene,
October's gold and amber stream.

GUARD THY LIPS.

OH, when harsh and hasty words arise,
And clouds of vexation dim the eyes,
And anger begins to settle down,
And the face puts on a sullen frown ;
When wrathful thoughts rush quickly up,
Oh, dash aside the poisoned cup,
       And guard thy lips !

Guard them, lest, in an unguarded hour,
They should utter, beyond thy power,
Words to wound some loving heart,
Perhaps, a lasting scar impart;
Inevitable words when once they're spoken,
Nothing can heal the heart they've broken,
       Then, guard thy lips !

EYES.

THERE'S no feature of the human face,
No peculiar air or winning grace,
That comprehends so much, yet so little tells,
As these deep, unfathomable wells :
We look to read vexation or surprise,
From the fountain of those orbs we prize.

Secrets, locked in portals of the heart,
Eyes help wonderfully to impart :
Of many eyes of many hues,
I've a choice : tell it ? I refuse.
Of the many eyes that smile or frown,
I'll not say 'tis black or brown.

It may be neither, but 'tis true,
'Tis one of which there are but few ;
It looketh kindly on God's creatures all,
Nor spurneth one tho' it be small ;
Their depths a volume of truth express,
Their color—but that I'll leave for you to guess.

LONG ENGAGEMENTS.

OH ! the long engagement on firm philosophy doth stand,
  Nor from that firmness should it e'er depart,
Ah, fair one, beware that when you bestow your hand,
  You are ready, too, to give your heart ;
Prepared to surrender it without retrieve,
That you may ne'er o'er that disposal grieve.

Be it carefully stored within the chamber of the mind forever,
  In this scandalous age of turmoil and strife,
Better be a contented " old maid " with no odious chain to sever,
  Than to be a miserable, unhappy wife ;
Be cautious of that step which may to outside counsel tend,
A step, in brief, to require the advice of a—" Mutual Friend."

Wary and deliberate, then, not a matrimonial rush so fast,
  Better now struggle through a year of heartache (?)
Than thread a life with clouds of misery o'ercast,
  Beholding repentance gush forth "too late;"
Better, though impatiently, some days of meditation waste,
Than repent, at leisure, for a marriage in haste.

Oh, the sad, sad dawning when that bitter truth awake,
  That Love hath forsaken his vine-wreathed bower,
The o'erwhelming grief that clusters round that sad "too late,"
  In its first dark and drenching shower:
Banish the short engagement, that paths with sorrow set,
That yes once said, may e'er be *yes*, without regret.

SEPTEMBER.

THE summer e'en in this eventful city has swiftly glided by,
  Leaving each heart its sorrow or joy to tell,
And each heart knows what in its hidden chambers lie,
  As summer biddeth earth farewell.
I would not cloud, for a moment, the sun of another's life,
  Only my own crowding thoughts express;
In this world where there's so much inevitable strife,
  'Tis not idle fancy to candidly confess,
That amid the sunshine and shower, the frown and smile,
There's scenes little actually worth one's while—
But this is for thee, absent friend, I would not give thee sorrow,
Though the world seems dark to-day, it may be light to-morrow.

CHICAGO, September 1, 1874.

THE MESSAGE I WOULD LEAVE.

I'm very sick, mamma, put your hand upon my breast,
I feel that I may die in the Garden City of the West,
My voice is weak. and trembling, blurs come before my eye,
I may recover, but take this message, lest that I should die :
A message for yourself, mamma, I leave it first of all,
Do not weep for me, mother, if death should chance to call;
Think of me as past to a warmer, more congenial spot,
Where storms of sorrow and tempests enter not ;
Conduct our plans, just as if I'd lived, you know,
From those bright realms I'll look upon the scene below :
Tell Willard for cousie's sake to have noble aims in view,
To walk the path that's harmless, nor deviate from the true:
And all my friends, where e'er they are, if I should die,
Give them this—my last good-bye.

CHICAGO, August 21, 1874.

A WOMAN'S HEART.

Miss Meddlesome who tries God's plans, and those of man,
Ever and anon with prying eyes to scan,
Admits one thing from her cautious eye apart,
And cries indignantly, " A woman's heart !"

Just as she thinks its contents nicely read,
Lo! she finds herself entirely misled;
A wonder more than mechanism of art—
Something ne'er read—a woman's heart!

Within its secret chambers there may lie
Joys or sorrows closely veiled from human eye,
An unsolved mystery from all eyes apart,
Read it if you can—a woman's heart!

The winning smile, and laugh so joyous glad,
May conceal feelings sorrowful and sad,
And the pensive brow and downcast look
Are alike an unread, a closéd book!

Dim want and woe, dark toil and care,
May have marred a face of beauty rare,
And love or hate may have played a part;
'Tis never read—a woman's heart!

Perchance the fitful pallor or vivid blush,
May give hope and courage quite a rush;
But don't think you've read it, not e'en in part,
That mystic problem, a woman's heart?

THE STEPMOTHER'S CHAIR.

FROM " FORGET-ME-NOT."

To those who are contemplating connubial bliss,
A word of kind advice is offered, it is this :
Consider the all-important step you're about to take,
And be sure you're sensing the responsibilities it awake,
For behold your future happiness at stake !
There is no half-way, 'tis a life of joy or one of woe,
Lies in the path toward which you go ;
Your thoughts into the bosom of Contemplation throw,
To study o'er your advancing fate,
Pauses in time save stumbles late :
Direct your attention to the monitor Beware,
For grief precedes you to the stepmother's chair !

Joys *may seem* waiting there for you,
And bright faced pleasures may seem in view,
But minute skeins of happiness you will see,
When once a stepmother you've come to be ;
Experience with this verdict must agree ;
Though the future look e'er so bright and fair,
Sorrow and trouble are lurking there,
Bound with the iron bands of care ;
Though Joy his fairest roses seem to strew,
The green-eyed Monster's there before you,
An e'er faithful monitor is Beware,
And he suspiciously eyes the stepmother's chair !

It is a step in which seriousness has a share,
Alas! it is no trivial affair
To take the step despite all who may entreat,
That leads you to that burdened seat,
Where discontent and opposition meet;
The mystic Nymph of Fate, behold her stand,
Striving for admittance at your right hand;
Portraying reality sketches, behold her plead!
That you'll lift up your eyes and read;
Pause, then, to scan the truth before your eyes,
Nor wake, too late, to a dread surprise—
But, hark! he nudges you—the monitor—Beware,
Look, he cries, Distress has sat down in the stepmother's chair!

DROP A TEAR FOR THAT LONE, LITTLE ONE.

OH, fortune's favorite, when at night you gather round
    Your fireside, snug and warm,
Think of the lone one who has not yet found
    A shelter from the blinding storm.
When the soft Æolian harp-strings you hear,
    As gently around you they play,
Oh, be merciful, and drop one pitiful tear,
    For that lone one in the wide world astray!
With no house but the lonely, cheerless street,
No kind friends to welcome, and none to greet!
Let sympathy flood up, gushingly, let it come,
And, oh, drop a tear for that lone, little one!

LOST STAR OF THE NIGHT.

For a brief space I enjoyed thy radiant light,
Ere thou wert gone, lost Star of the Night!
    Happy moments, suddenly o'er;
Too bright! too bright! they could not stay;
Yet hope sheddeth a faint little ray,
    That Time my lost Star will restore.
Though I may have toiled thro' many a weary day,
One hand moveth the world's machinery aright,
And I may behold my lost Star of the Night!

Methinks no brighter moments ever were seen,
Than those that checkered my life with green;
    Swift-winged they flitted by;
From out the past I recall them now,
With aching heart and throbbing brow,
    And tears stealing to my eye,
Weakness I fain would not allow:
But when the darkness is deep, soon comes the light,
Return, oh, my lost Star of the Night

NELLIE.

O'ER the fallow lea and upland lawn,
You would see our Nellie at early dawn,
And truly an added charm seemed lent,
Where'er her gladsome footsteps went.

With the gentle sway of an angel's wing,
A thousand joys to our life she'd bring;
The earth was flooded with gold and green,
When God removed our one sunbeam.

HE HAD BUT ONE FAULT.

HIGH-BORN and wealthy was proud old Col. Lee,
His home was in the distinguished city of B.,
Ten years gone by his wife had died,
And an only daughter was his stay—his pride.

Muriel, I must admit, was wondrously fair,
Not because romances prate of pink cheeks and golden hair;
Not the story that's grown insipid and olden,
Her cheeks had no pink, her hair, no hue of golde

Au contraire, 'twas straight, and of a pale brown hue,
Her eyes were gray, instead of violet blue,
But a lovelier face one doesn't often see,
And none saw, but loved sweet Muriel Lee.

One autumn, the son of Col. Lee's old college friend,
Came a few weeks with them to spend;
Victor St. Clare was of genuine French descent,
While an Appollo-like form to his beauty lent.

Warmly received, for none but Muriel had he eyes.
And plainly she his every look did prize,
Till, at length, one day the finale came,
Fair Muriel for his own he'd claim.

They wanted but the blessing of Col. Lee,
But that they knew could never be;
He had favored the son of his old friend,
But had never dreamed of such an end.

But why did he plead, and plead in vain,
He was of high birth, bore an honored name;
An esteemed friend's only son—
His faults how few—he had but *one.*

But that one of woful misery was a sign,
He sometimes took a glass of wine.
I forbear to picture the meeting at dead of night,
The whispered words—the hurried flight!

     *   *   *   *   *   *   *   *   *   *

" Ten years, ten years, and can it be,
Since I resigned the name of Lee ?
Ah, yes, for 'tis ten years this very night—
The well feigned plot, the cautious flight!

" Ten years, and can it possibly be ten ?
Dear Victor ! how beautiful he look then,
But the years—oh, no—the *cursed wine*
Has changed his form, so tall and fine !

" My heart was warm, and, oh, how light !
My trembling form in a robe of white ;
The clergyman, his wife and daughter, there,
' I wish you joy, Mrs. St. Clare.'

" My father's pleading voice, his earnest way,
' Muriel, you'll surely rue this day—'
But why recall that far-off scene,
That comes like a vague, fantastic dream ?

" Where is he should be here this anniversary eve ?
How can I the sad truth, tho' I know, believe ?
But, wait, I'll hush Fredie sound to sleep,
Then, I'll look him out in the street.

* * * * * * * * *

" Hark ! what fearful noise is that I hear ?
Those deafening peals that reach my ear ?—
Six o'clock ? surely, then, I've lost time,
For the last I heard it strike was nine.

" Fredie, where's my child, my precious babe?
How could I thus stupidly have laid?—
Oh, he's yonder on his drunken father's arm!
Oh, God protect my babe from harm!

" Victor, my darling, come home with me,
Come, come with your own Muriel Lee,
Oh, do not sneer at my prayers and tears,
Why fall my entreaties on deaf ears?"

Rude boys are stoning the drunken man there,
And one strikes the temple of Muriel St. Clare,
Thro' the air it comes with a buzzing sound,
And she staggers senseless to the ground!

A confuséd noise, a man rushes thro' the street,
On comes the tread of tramping feet!
Col. Lee emerges from an unseen quarter,
And bends o'er the form of his lifeless daughter!

Little Fredie, Muriel's baby boy,
Is taken to the house of luxury, but no longer joy,
The tale of many and many another,
The babe soon lies beside its mother.

And as Col. Lee sits musing o'er other days,
O'er so much that seems a perfect daze,
Piercing shrieks fly through the air,
'Tis the maniac voice of Victor St. Clare!

Ah, turn not scornfully away, my skeptic friend,
Would that I could this tale more pleasing end,
In that perilous course, *now* is the time to halt,
Beware, beware of that one delusive fault!

CILOME.

SHE comes, at morn, at noon, at eventide,
Lovely Cilome is at our side;
If the day be cloudy, or be it fair,
She leaveth not her invalid chair;
Yet much of life to her is bright,
But she's fading slowly from our sight.
We love her, oh, so deeply, purely!
Yet we clasp her not securely,
For the fair cheek grows daily whiter,
And the dark eye clear and brighter;
Though around her our affections twine,
Soon must we our pet resign.
Once she was gay from morn till night,
But she's fading slowly from our sight.
We love her, yet know that a better home
Awaits our beauteous, lovely Cilome.

HEARTS AND CLOTHES.

A SUIT of broadcloth sure is well,
    A watch of eighteen carats gold;
    But can such appendage please the eye
      If the heart be stony cold?
Who can but admire a heart where inherent beauties lay,
Tho' it be covered o'er with a suit of coarse sheep's grey?

    Though to admire a silk of soft, sky-blue,
      Of itself may be no harm,
    If the inward motives be not true
      It loseth every charm.
The lustrous splendor fades from silk so soft,
If there be no pure aspirations beneath to soar aloft.

    Whate'er the external dress may be,
      Though many a jewel round it hovers,
    Should we not e'er search first
      To see what heart it covers?
For many a tinsel from Fashion's expansive store,
Hideous deformities, perchance, may cover o'er.

DEAR MOTHER, I'M THINKING OF THEE.

DREARILY, drearily, snow and rain beat,
Forming together a dismal sleet,
And behind a cloud the moon has withdrawn,
  E'en Luna's smiles I no longer can see,
Nothing cheerful around me to dawn ;
  But, dear mother, I *may* think of thee.

And a star of miraculous brightness,
Sheds at once a calm, brilliant lightness,
Before the eyes that no slumbers trace,
  Emiting, oh, such a gladsome gleam,
For directly I see thy patient face,
  O'er the waste of miles between.

Ah, mother, thou lovest me, and it's hard to tell,
If another will ever love me as well ;
And strangely float thy words, sweet mother,
  That oft thou hast spoken to me.
That " At best the love of another
  Slight to a mother's must be."

Dear mother, tried and trusted friend,
A prayer to Heaven doth now ascend ;
And far away to-night though thou art,
  Our Father'll be near unto thee ;
And thus bound together in heart,
  Dear mother, I'm thinking of thee.

THE WHITE DRESS.

"ANOTHER white dress, I do declare,
I think it is too absurd,"
Observed with an unrelenting air,
The haughty Mrs. Furd.

But there are sorrowful hearts to-day,
And mourning on West street to-night,
For they've closed the eyes of Minnie Gray,
And robed her form in white.

Alas, who would not dress with care
That graceful, lifeless form?
She'll never want another share,
Reserve the frown and scorn.

LOVE THAT'S LOVE FOREVER.

LOVE! the word grates unmusically on the ear!
Yet 'tis a word should ever sound dear;
But where is the love in this cold, unromantic age,
That fades not soon from memory's page?

Where is there a love like Jacob's of yore,
Seven years' labor, and then seven more?
In what kind of a channel does love now glide?
Who'd labor half of fourteen years for a bride?
Where is that love that perishes never?
And where is that love that is love forever?

Love! there it is glowing vividly on pages of fiction,
Set forth with brilliancy minus restriction;
Love! we see it in those blissful, imaginary scenes,
Away in Fancy's bright castle of dreams;
But when we come back from those fairy skies,
With stern Reality before our eyes,
Back to this stage of struggle and strife,
We look in vain for that love in grim real life;
For where is that love that perishes never?
And where is that love that is love forever?

A gentle word, a kindly act, a winning smile,
May personate love for a little while;
The silent handclasp, the thrilling touch,
That seem to say, " I love thee much; "
Soul-speaking eyes, a voice that trembles slightly,
And says, " I do not love thee lightly ;"
And, oh, beware ! for Cupid a Counterfeit sends,
And rarely his stately presence lends;
For where is that love that perishes never?
And where is that love that is love forever?

Ofttimes a *fancy* for *love* is mistaken,
Sad indeed, as the fact in the future awaken!
Smiling angels ne'er look down from above,
To sanction a limpy apology for love:
Think *such* a heart adamant, do you? so hard!
Of all inherent flexibility debarred;
But if love with memory's dews is e'er wet,
I reiterate, true love can never forget;
For where is that love that perishes never?
And where is that love that is love forever?

ARIEL AND LITTLE NELL.

'NEATH the Willow at the well,
    In those by-gone, golden days,
Sat Ariel and little Nell,
    And shared each other's plays.

While he reached manhood proud and free,
    Rare loveliness on *her* fell,
And still beneath that Willow-tree
    Sat Ariel and little Nell.

Days passed like bright sunbeams,
    Draughts from joy's deepest well
Brightened the youthful dreams
    Of Ariel and little Nell.

But a message flew o'er the wires—
  They spoke their sad farewell,
Of their hopes and fond desires,
  'Neath the Willow at the well.

Their parting mingled with sighs and tears,
  " Sad railroad accident! and —" oh, well,
They looked in less than two short years,
  On the graves of Ariel and little Nell.

Close beside his grave they laid her,
  'Neath the Willow at the well,
And gently the fall leaves stir,
  O'er the graves of Ariel and little Nell.

GIVE ME THE " DINNER OF HERBS."

Tho' all luxurious ornaments hung round,
That e'er in Wealth's domains are found,
Must e'er arise dissention's sound,
    Give me the " dinner of herbs."

Rather than clouds of discontent should prey,
Growing denser from day to day,
With seldom a smile that's cheerful or gay,
    Give me the " dinner of herbs."

Rather than admit a frown, though slight,
Implying that something isn't right;
Than take one inch from peaceful light,
 Give me the " dinner of herbs."

Though a stalled ox for a moment please the taste,
Who life's happiness would waste,
Or o'er it put a gilded paste?
 Give me the "dinner of herbs."

Must we choose between the two,
My friend, I will not speak for you,
But deliberately, calm and true,
 Give me the " dinner of herbs."

OUR BETTER HOME.

OH, why bestow upon our love and best affection,
 And hug as a miser hugs his treasure,
A world which promises no protection
 'Gainst uncertain life and pleasure;
And though some joys we grasp by the wayside,
 They're a transient gift, a loan,
Not till we've crossed the mystic tide,
 Shall we behold our better home.

It hath been said " this beautiful world of ours,"
 But there is one more bright,
Where bloom far more lasting flowers,
 Than ever greet our sight;

There we may spend the endless ages,
  With Jesus, our Father's son,
Not till we've turned life's fickle pages,
  Shall we behold our better home.

We're borne along on Time's untiring wing,
  Soon must we loose our hold
On every vain and earthly thing ;
  Then, what, alas, is gold
And wealth beside a Higher approbation ?
  Tho' Fame and Honor round us shone,
We were the same of lowly station,
  Till we reach our better home.

I've gazed at the distant dazzling moon,
  And wandered by the lakelet clear,
In the balmy month of June,
  When angel voices seemed hovering near,
And His presence filled the air,
  And 'mid all the beauties there that shone
Up rose whispers of a world more fair,
  It is our better home.

Then, let us keep this thought in view
  As we journey on our way,
When this fleeting life is through,
  There is a brighter day,
If we strive to enter the straight gate in,
  Thro' the means which God hath given ;
Know in this world of strife and sin,
  Our better home's in Heaven.

A DOUBLE LIFE.

I ENTERED the palatine mansion grand,
  Perceived a mildew in the air,
Though elegance on every hand
  Sat smiling 'mid the grandeur there.
She who came forward with a smile
  Was honored Lady Blée,
And yet, beneath the hand of style
  Was something stored away.

A picture of the dim, far-distant past,
  That highly she once did prize;
A picture with misty shadows overcast,
  And hid from human eyes.
A seat beside a well-sweep oaken,
  A coat of homespun gray,
A pledge that should ne'er béen broken,
  Alas, a title was in the way!

Then the hand of ivory whiteness
  Was browned in summer's sun,
And the heart was full of lightness,
  To hail the days, ah, every one!
Now the shadows that o'er her lay
  Showed care and sorrow rife:
Oh, who, e'en to be Lady Blée,
  Would lead a double life?

A PROPHECY.

A WOMAN o'er whose low, bowed head,
   Three-score years have rolled,
And gray and silver have found a bed,
   Where rested auburn braid and fold.
She recalls through a channel blotted by years,
   Dreams of the vague, far past,
While Faith, not Fancy, quietly rears
   Bright castles that may last.
With resignation she looks to Heaven,
   Grateful for joys that proved so fleeting,
And for that mite of fruitful leaven,
   That signals their future meeting;
And she is happy with her day-dreams
   Lying shattered all around,
And Memory wandering o'er scenes
   That cause a sigh profound.
Wonder and surprise may mingle,
   At this lonely woman's choice,
That she should live unloved and single,
   Away from kindred voice.
Unloved? Ah, no; for children of mirth and glee,
   With flowers to form and dolls to dress,
Fondle unrebuked around her knee,
   With soft and sweet caress;

And the velvety hands of the city maiden,
    And toil-brown palms of the country lass,
When their hearts with sorrow are laden,
    Are reached to her for a comfort-pass ;
And she, searching Memory's spectral hall,
    Banishing all cares of her own,
Draws thence a word of advice for all,
    That her early years hath sown.
With such a degree of patience she listens
    To their youthful troubles laid,
That her eye with tears oft glistens,
    At the words, " What a good ' old maid '!"
And to her the aged, bowed with years,
    Come with their heavy grief,
And receive the balmy word that cheers,
    And gives to the mind relief.
She finds " old maids " can be of u tility after all ;
    Though not wives and mothers,
They can answer the piteous call,
    And starving cry of others ;
And Fortune's favored hand that's laid
    With Fate's mystic chimes agreed,
Within the home of this "old maid,"
    Benefits those who need.
There's a wealth of house-plants and garden flowers,
    For the unfortunate an ample space ;
And in her thoughtful, leisure hours,
    The pen is her companion fair,
Many a long and weary hour beguiling ;

Yea, after a life's struggle and strife,
She grasps the Genius that cast his smiling
    O'er the early morning of her life;
And turns one tho't adown the grassy slopes,
    To bid a long, a last farewell.
O'er her dreams and dead purposes
    The heart no longer may swell;
Nor eye kindle with joyous pride,
    At some fond, lingering glance;
Bubbles that float o'er life's youthful tide,
    Break as the stream advance.
Hark! the air itself seems almost stilled,
    At the close of these fancied lines;
Will the prophecy be fulfilled,
    For her who pens these rhymes?

THE IMPRESS ON THE SAND.

HE sat, a child of five years old,
    And carv'd with his fat and dimpled hand,
Pictures, he called brave and bold,
    In the bed of scorching sand.

Next day he went to see his pictures fair,
    And, thoughtful, for a moment did he stand,
For the pictures were no longer there,
    But their impress was on the sand.

Thus the pictures we're carving from day to day,
  Our utmost thought and care demand,
For, though the original be swept away,
  The impress will ever stand.

AND THE YEARS GO BY.

Then the varied seasons come and go,
There's summer's sun and winter's snow;
To some they bring akin to unbroken joy,
To others, misfortunes that hope destroy;
Some seem rushing headlong thro' the world,
Grasping whate'er in their reach is hurl'd;
Some, striving with neighbors to vie;
And that's the way the years go by.

Some are flitting blithely to and fro,
Culling all the best as they go;
Here the marriage bells are ringing,
While lov'd friends bright gifts are bringing;
There, not a mile, perchance, between,
Behold a sad, contrasting scene!
Death a fair, youthful mourner would crave,
As she weeps over a new-made grave.

While some life's voyage are just beginning,
With hope of future joys winning,
Others have swallowed the dregs of life's bitter cup,
And would fain sit down not to rise up;

Verily each day brings its joy or care,
Its hours clouded, or its hours fair;
Some gayly laugh while others sigh,
And that's the way the years go by.

AT THE CLOSE OF SUMMER'S LAST DAY.

THOU art many a mile from here at this twilight hour,
   And, I, oh, I'm so weary and faint,
Yet I'll bring one picture from Memory's bower,
   And bid Poesy endeavor to paint;
And canst thou not guess what that picture must be,
Or doubt for a moment 'tis a picture of thee?
Just as the sun glides adown the west,
   I think of thee, absent friend, far away,
As I watch the beams with their golden crest,
   Shining at the close of summer's last day;
(And foretelling the speedy arrival of autumnal air,
Methinks they point at the snow white dress I wear;)
And down in the channel of by-gone weeks,
   Is a picture that long must last,
It hath its gray and its golden streaks,
   And they form a sweet, sad contrast;
We met, and kindled affection twined round each heart,
Gray streaks the golden—'tis when we part.

CHICAGO, August 31, 1874.

SUSAN JANE.

A HOOD in winter, and shaker in summer days,
  Covered the silvery head,
  " Old and cross " the children said:
Old fashioned and queer in all her ways,
    Every day she went her round,
    Picking up aught that was to be found,
    From rise of morn till set of sun,
    She could not say her work was done ;
From day-break, at early morn, onward went the weary form,
    Up and down the city lane,
    The half-bent form of Susan Jane.

There never occurred the thought that she once was young,
    That the same wrinkled, old face was fair,
    And bronze those silvery locks of hair ;
Only that an unfathomable mystery round her hung :
    From homes of luxury comes bright light,
    Tho' 'tis still but the hour of twilight—
    That hut with splicéd door and broken pane,
    Behold the home of Susan Jane !
A sad tale it is to be told, of this creature so shrunken and old,
    A blighted life, but there's no reproach or stain,
    On the heart and character of Susan Jane.

The morn was piercing cold, keen, frosty was the air,
   The piteous object was not on her wonted round,
   Within was not a stir, not a sound ;
They broke the wooden door and found beside her empty chair,
   Clasping a miniature with many a stain,
   The lifeless form of Susan Jane :
   A face of girlish beauty, 'side one manly bold.
   Alas, the sad sequel it unfold !
A fair and young, but humble, girl—her lover, the son of a
      mercenary earl,
   Deceit and fraud to part the train,
   Such is the story of Susan Jane.

LOVE OF A LIFETIME.

SARATOGA ! delightful spot ! where cares are banished from the
   mind,
   Where time flies all too swift to measure,
Where many for idle hours pastime and amusement find,
   And drown their perplexing tho'ts in pleasure :
Saratoga ! how many a memorable scene before thee flies,
How many a romance buried in thy bosem lies !

September and the popular season of resort is o'er,
   Crowds of guests for respective homes are starting ;
In a rustic bower where many have met before,
   Sat two speaking of the coming day—the day of parting ;
A maiden whom nineteen years of joy had beautified,
A noble form of as many years and ten was at her side.

"A meeting and a parting, how near they come together—
I love you," said he, "dearest one, I know,
With a love that will grow brighter and still brighter ever,
That time shall but tinge with an ever-reviving glow."
But the brilliant heiress had heard many a tale by love before,
And questioned were *this* not the same smoothly varnished o'er.

Still Conscience was pleading for the love and music in her ear,
What her words would have been none e'er may know ;
Her dark eyes turned to him, in one there stood a tear,
Three words escaped, in accents firm and low,
"Have you considered "—a convulsive gasp—hands clasp'd, as
if to pray,
And in his loving arms her lifeless body lay.

Oft came before his eyes smiles from fairy forms in floating dress,
But the wild tumult of his heart was never stilled,
'Twas one to him, for no amount of flattery or caress
Could fill the heart that *she* had filled.
The years have cycled round fifty times and nine,
Still he clings with fond affection to the lost love of a lifetime.

THE SAILOR'S WIFE.

"AND I've stood to-day and watched the White Cloud float away,
Away, away, o'er the stormy sea,
One true heart it bore from me ;
Ah, mayn't come anxiety and pain, ere I see it float back again.

" Bravely he steeled his heart, as we stood on the deck to part,
 But more than all my sobs and cries,
 Spoke those two tearless eyes ;
Alas ! I ask, pitiless sea, return again my love to me.

" While out on the moaning deep, his lone vigil he'll keep,
 I shall pray for and await him here,
 Perchance oft with trembling and fear ;
Hidden from my nearest relation, only One can give consolation.

" Yes, there is comfort to be had, e'en though I am sad,
 The same Eye looks on the stormy sea,
 That here, lovingly, watcheth o'er me ;
Life would be, oh, how black ! should the White Cloud never
  come back.

" Gone from dearest friend and relation, to meet trial and
  temptation ;
 But One his protector will be,
 Far out on the boisterous sea ;
I here wait and yearn that the White Cloud in due time return."

Years have gone, twenty and nine, her face is old before its time ;
 Fainter and fainter her lamp of life burned,
 And the White Cloud has never returned :
She's a maniac, and, wildly, you may hear her say,
" I know I saw it sail away, and 'twill surely come back some day."

THE GRAIN OF MUSK.

YEAR after year hath the wee particle lain,
Still, strong the perfume of the little grain :
So, when we have passed from care and pain,
Will the record of our acts and deeds remain.

TIRED OF LIFE.

(REAL.)

HIS voice was piteous, and his face was thin,
  As he begged for a morsel of bread ;
But no one welcomed him in ;
They pushed him away, and the sin
  Silently recoiled on their head.

" Kind gentlemen, give me a dime,"
  And he heaved a heart-rending sigh ;
" Alas, when fair fortune once was mine,
I've given, ah, how many a time !
  Now I'm starving and longing to die.

"Sir, loan me your knife, if you please;'
Tightly he clasped that fatal knife·
Ere the rash hand one could seize,
His sorrowful mind was at ease—
His own hand had ended his life.

These words, reader, I would say to you,
Turn not the beggar away,
For this sad tale is only too true,
And is only one of all that accrue,
Then speak to him kindly for aye.

LINES.

TO B. B. RUSSELL, PUBLISHER, BOSTON,

On receiving his present of a volume of Poems, entitled, "From Shore to Shore."

INSPIRING gift! with gratitude I press it to my heart,
And fondly clasp it o'er and o'er;
Beauteous gems within, that golden thoughts impart,
Of a promised bright, unfading Shore!
Gratitude that by tongue or pen cannot be told,
For a treasure richer far to me than gold.

And may it oft my thoughts to Heaven uplift,
  From hence o'er mountain and river.
And gazing on the choice-bound gift,
  May I not forget the giver;
Your kindness to an unpretending author shown
  Shall elicit thoughts from her distant valley home.

And know that oft o'er each word, as o'er a feast,
  I shall dwell with thoughtful care!
My treasured and glowing emblem of the east,
  That to my far-off home I bear!
Grateful, too, that when here I can no longer tarry,
I hence your kindly wishes carry!

And when to this city I shall bid farewell,
  Accept my own, for I shall leave behind,
Though no verbal word or token tell,
  Wishes of the purest, sincere kind;
While these words will ever flit my eyes before,
Remember yon fair perennial Shore!

And Fancy in her meandering way may dally,
  To picture sometimes the charms,
Of a delightful and charming valley,
  In Oriskany's fair arms;
To picture, too, oft before my doting eyes,
  The pages of the book I prize.

Here I came to a city all unknown,
    Alike unknown to any,
But ere two short weeks have flown,
    I find my friends are, many.
I hold memorials linked with kind words spoken,
But above I prize this lasting, star-gemmed token.

Once more my priceless gem that naught can measure,
    With inherent beauties that cannot perish,
My prized but yet unfathomed treasure,
    Thy worth I e'er must cherish;
And when life's rough voyage at last is o'er,
    We shall have passed " from Shore to Shore."
Boston, August 22, 1873.

I FORGET THEE NOT.

TO AGNES P————.

Does the sun e'er tire of rising and going down again ?
Or the moon of looking down at night o'er field and plain ?
Just so are my untiring thoughts the same.

Tho' river and gulf now spread out 'tween thee and me,
And though we're wide apart on Life's great sea,
Yet no more, my friend, do I forget thee.

Is it tiresome to bear thee constantly in my mind ?
Ah, what easier burden could I hope to find ?
'Tis the lightest surely, and the dearest kind.

Thou art e'er in the mind's recess, whether I would or not,
And in the heart's garden, thou hast a warm, warm spot,
And the roses whisper, thou ne'er shalt be forgot.

The days are dull and stupid, since thou left the city,
Hours of *ennui* filled with nothing gay or witty;
Oh, say, why art thou gone ? 'tis such a pity!

Dull are the streets where thou wert wont to walk;
Monotonous the circles in which thou used to talk;
And in our social gatherings there comes many a balk.

But this thou know, where e'er I am, where e'er my lot,
Whether in the gay mansion, or the humble cot,
Remember that I still forget thee not.

ON THE SHORE OF LAKE MICHIGAN.

PRELUDE.

Gone the Spring, and the smiles of winsome June
   Deck again this gladsome earth of ours,
And gay birds sing in a flute-like tune,
   Of the merry bells and blushing flowers;

When the scorching sun, without any pity,
　Pours down from the western sky,
Oh, to leave the din of the dusty city,
　And come where the cool lake breeze sweeps by.

Away from the hurry and worry, and toil and care,
　While the world's confusion pauses not,
Oh, we'll leave it all a brief respite to share,
　In the quiet of this beautiful spot ;
While up through the vestibule of the Past,
　Memory swiftly, but surely, doth rake,
Bringing hence sunshine and shadow so fast,
　On the shore of the placid lake.

And the scepter of the past and the Future's shade,
　Or joy gone by, and light to come,
In the bosom of the lake together are laid,
　And there find a peaceful home ;
Here, by the side of the lake, to-day,
　With a chance for deep thought given,
How many a prayer for those far away,
　Is borne on the breezes to heaven.

Here, to the side of the calm lake, towards night,
　Come the aged whose heads are gray,
And the young, some of whose lives are bright,
　And others who've once been gay ;
And some go back o'er mountain and valley,
　To muse on some happy hour of life ;
Others, tho' o'er by-gone scenes they rally,
　Recall little but struggles and strife.

Here to the side of the smooth floating lake,
   Come those whose burdens are heavy to bear,
And those whose hearts are ready to break,
   From a sorrow locked up with care ;
And others breathe soft air at the lakeside,
   Who have never known a grief,
Nor a passing shadow on Life's great tide,
   Nor a sorrow however brief.

Those for whom Hope treasures no bright to-morrow,
   Seek this sequestered nook ;
Those whose troubles come before they borrow,
   On these tranquil waves doth look ;
Those whose clouds have ne'er a silver lining,
   Paths hedged with doubt and all uncertain,
With not a ray of bright light shining,
   Behind the Future's mystic curtain.

Here came the haughty, and here the proud,
   Here, too, the meek and modest seek retreat,
Low spoken words and laughter loud,
   Together at the lakeside meet;
While boisterous words from some lips fall,
   Others with knowledge and wisdom double,
Rarely to conversation turn at all,
   Because of some impending trouble.

And, beauteous Lake, blended with thy dream,
   Is the sweet and vacant smile,
Wove o'er many a fond love scene,
   Beneath thy gaze the while ;

Revenge, vowed the recreant and dilatory lover,
  Has reached thy hearing straight,
And thy broad, blue waves are a cover,
  For the tale I here relate.

*   *   *   *   *   *

The month was May, and the evening calm and still,
  A young girl of slender form and beauty rare
Stepped from her palatial home, sped down the little hill,
  To catch a breath of the soft, balmy air.
Quickly she reached the rose-hung, mossy gate,
  " My intention, I believe, I will forsake;
I only tho't of coming here, but its not late,
  I'll take a few steps toward the breezy lake.'

And ere Ivonne Leslie was the least aware,
  Her home was hid from sight;
Sha turned to retrace her steps, and there
  Beheld what caused her to start in fright.
Her senses reeled, her blood turned cold,
  Her hands clenched in a convulsive way,
O'er her horror in blackest volumes rolled,
  Before her a seeming lifeless body lay.

Her first tho't was to run and leave the scene behind,
  Then a second resolve was taken,
Scanning the channels of her bewildered mind,
  She bade her energies all awaken;

Suppose, tho't she, 'twas my only darling brother,
　Wrecked here at this untimely hour,
No kind sister near, or fond, devoted mother,
　I'll rescue him ; it's in my power.

" Who knows but he's a robber, fierce and bold,
　Ah, Fear, just stand back a moment, please,
For I have jewels of my own, and gold,
　If he's in need I'll give him these ;
It seems so sad, he looks so fair and young,
　Such an innocent and truthful face,
Could one sinister or evil look e'er clung
　Round such comeliness and grace ? "

So saying, with low and cautious tread,
　She stooped by the youthful sleeper's side,
Raised carefully his dark brown head,
　And boldly the complaints of Fear defied ;
Suddenly his eyes unclosed and gazed into her own,
　Then stared mazed and wonderingly around,
Solving where he had by Fate been blown,
　And by whom he had been found.

" An angel dropped from heaven, I guess—
　But, stay, it may be a spy sent out,
Ah, lady, your countenance is angelic, I confess,
　And yet—excuse me, I'm full of fear and doubt.
How came you here I beg to ask, and why,
　If you are a lady, *true*, without disguise,
Will you not in pity help me die,
　And hide me from mortal eyes ? "

"As for your doubts and fears, just let them go,
    Henceforth I'm your friend with your consent;
Your staunch friend, and not your foe,
    So ease your mind and be content;
But I cannot help you, however, to die,
    For I want you to live and think life a treasure;
Come now, papa's house is close by,
    And he'll welcome you there with pleasure."

"Ah, lady, you're kind, but you surely don't know
    That I've tarnished my once pure name,
In an unguarded hour dealt a murderous blow,
    And stamped myself with a murder's stain.
Ah, gentle lady," as Ivonne shuddered and shrank away,
    "I thought you'd hardly wish to take me in,
But I could'nt go on in the drama-like play
    Without telling you of my sin."

Ivonne with shame and agony bowed down,
    Pressed her hand to her burning brow,
Then said with the semblance of a frown,
    "I'll not forsake you now.
Now, we'll go, but let me tell you first,
    You keep quiet and I'll tell the story,
With thrilling little details nurst,
    Relating to your honor and your glory.

"It may be wrong, but his confession in my ears was emptied,
    And his countenance is frank and clear,
A mystery! he may have been too greatly tempted,
    I'll protect him regardless of all fear;

Should they trace him I'd be in danger,
  But love and affection are already rife,
Fate has guided me to this mysterious stranger,
  I'll risk myself to save his life."

Months at the Leslie mansion flew away,
  Summer had rolled into the past,
October tinged the earth with gray,
  And her realms with sombre hues o'ercast.
Within the grape-vine arbor laid the rescued Clarence Osgood,
  And with eyes pure vacancy roaming o'er;
Before him with a wildly beating heart Ivonne Leslie stood,
  He murmured a name he'd uttered oft before.

  "Alice," and with a bounding heart of pain,
    Ivonne knelt by her admired darling's side,
  And listened closely as he breathed "Alice Lorraine,"
    "The deceitful little wretch," she cried,
  Then took back her words, for she was good at heart,
    Could she reproach a girl she'd never seen?
  "But," said she, "it's time for us to part,
    And *dream* of the parenthesis that's been.

  "For I can no longer stand, I know, to hear
    A name that I so much detest—
  A name that's become odious to my ear,
    Being by those sweet lips pressed;
  If I had only let him die that night
    Perhaps 'twould have all been better.
  Ah, wait, what is that looks so white?
    As I live it is a—yes, a letter.

"A letter, but of a far distant date,
  Penned by her own false, fair hand,
Ha, ha, would she share a murderer's fate,
  She knows not of that blighting brand?
I'll let her know it, then, when he is free,
  And cast aside in the world alone,
He may grow some time to think of me,
  Who for his life would lay down my own."

She hid the hated letter her dread returning,
  Lest he suddenly should awake,
With all the excitement in her burning,
  She sought the quiet lake;
A letter was written, directed to a fair Southern city,
  And then flung spitefully aside,
"Ivonne Leslie, it surely is a lamentable pity
  If you must beg to be a murderer's bride."

The words were hissed between her closed teeth,
  "I saved him from a path-dishonor paves"—
She rose, her feet sank underneath,
  She fell amid the dark and rushing waves;
A stranger saw her fall, and instantly he flew,
  Plunged into the water cold,
And forth the precious burden drew,
  With courage undaunted, bold.

In a swoon upon the sofa she was lain,
  Reviving she tho't of Clarence, not the hero brave,
Then she spied a card that bore the name
  Of him who took her from a watery grave;

She gave a cry, a start, and then fell back,
   " Louis Lorraine" was the name it bore ;
What unconnected link could Fate then lack,
   To be supplied by bringing him to their door?

And oft thereafter in the future did they meet,
   The envied Alice's brother pulled her from death's mouth
The romantic episode she might complete,
   And become a bride of the sunny South ;
No word of Alice or Osgood was spoke, howe'er,
   For the latter had crossed the ocean,
But oft from Ivonne broke an impetuous prayer
   For him, touched with deep emotion.

 *   *   *   *   *   *   *

Another month of May, the night is fair and clear,
   Ivonne Leslie stands by the lake again,
Recalls the night she found him here,
   Just a year ago, the night self-same.
She gazes at the smooth waves as they gently glide,
   Then heaves a sigh, draws her shawl more tight.
This time Louis Lorraine is sitting by her,
   While she fancies Clarence there to-night.

The wind blows softly—then more brisk,
   A storm is rising, they must return,
Shall he make the venture, run the risk,
   And his fate, good or bad, now learn?
Her snow white hands are clasped together,
   A hungry stare in the burning eyes,
Too statuesque he fears for love to sever,
   But he *must* attempt, and so he tries.

Words of love's lasting and sweet assurance,
  He poured at his heart's idol's feet,
She listened with ill-concealed endurance,
  Moved uneasily on her grassy seat.
She had pity, for alike she had respect,
  Liked him as the friend who'd sav'd her life,
But not a spark of that love could she detect,
  Due him from her were she his wife.

Many a time in past weeks she'd tho't of this,
  Dreamed it out and planned it o'er,
Concluded, too, that she should answer yes,
  From *gratitude*, but nothing more,
But the decisive moment now at hand,
  She felt her resolution break,
For lo! she stood away in a foreign land,
  Though sitting by that never-to-be-forgotten lake.

She loved another that was but too true ;
  And with her love so far away,
She felt that *his* must be unreal, too,
  That he'd meet his true love some day.
" Ah, I'll say my heart is across the ocean's tide,
  And you, my noble friend and brother,
Surely would not wish a heartless bride,
  Whose love is given to another.

" But no, Clarence would be implicated by that story,
  I'll do it better—I have it now ;
Go, wait my friend for fame and glory,
  To twine their arms around your brow.

I am myself too young to marry, and you're not old,
   Wait for two short years to flit around,
Another within your heart my place will hold,
   Your true love, I prophecy to then be found.

   *   *   *   *   *   *   *

A night in August of the ensuing fall,
   Ivonne sits by the lake in twilight gray.
In searching round, dreaming of no company at all,
   She spies a man and a maiden gay.
Slowly she raises the glass up to her eyes,
   Closes her lips, no sound comes out,
For the man is Clarence—the maiden—Alice, no doubt.

She turned, looked at the lake she might see no more.
   Swift hot tears her eyes did swell,
" My life has been shipwrecked on this shore,
   But I bid it now a last farewell.
I saved his life, refused a love as good as gold,
   To see him after his absence in a foreign land,
Renew that boyish fancy; to me indifferent and cold,
   But soon on foreign soil, I too, shall stand."

   *   *   *   *

The paper dropped from the cold and nerveless hand—
   Three years had swiftly flitted by,
When in that far and distant land,
   This paragraph met her eye:

The marriage of her only brother Wilbur,
  With Alice, youngest daughter of R. Lorraine,
A wealthy and prosperous Southern planter,
  Of ancient and honored name.

And the couples the happy pair attending,
  The name of Louis Lorraine, brother of the bride,
With Minnie, sister of Clarence Osgood, blending,
  Lifted a curtain revealing the mystified;
And Ivonne knew—and wish'd she'd kissed her,
  That the lovely girl with Clarance *that night,*
Was her brother's wife, his darling sister,
  It was a revelation of refulgent light!

    *   *   *   *

The White Star was ploughing thro' the waves,
  The winds were howling loud,
And fast beat the heart of the sailor braves,
  As they noticed each fierce and threatening cloud;
Tearful eyes gazed from cabin windows afar,
  And piteous sobs rent the midnight air,
And one there was in that doom'd White Star,
  Alone, and oh, so young and fair.

With long and jetty hair unbound,
  With eyes of haunting midnight hue,
With clasped hands, without a sound,
  She scanned the sickening view.

With blanching cheeks and paling lips Ivonne Leslie stood,
The blood seemed curdling in her heart.
A loved name trembled on her lips—"Clarence Osgood,"
A deafening shock, and the White Star rent apart.

She opened her eyes on board another ship, gallant and proud,
Felt herself supported in two strong arms,
A young lord on the Europe bound White Cloud
Had rescued her 'mid perilous alarms;
And the fair patient unconsciously won his heart,
With her his fond thot's were woven in connection;
With wealth, rank and title, would he part
Could he but gain her heart's affection.

On plashed the White Cloud o'er the foamy waves,
While Inna's new found friend clung to her side
Almost wishing they might find ocean graves,
If she could not be, alive, his bride;
And Inna essayed to let past hopes vanish
For his sake, to whom she owed her life,
But lo, a tumultuous pleading she could not banish,
For remembrance of an *undying* love was rife.

Love's confession and fond entreaty were in vain,
For Inna was too true to deceive another,
E'en though it gave his true heart pain,
And she clung firmly to her former lover;
"Oh," thought Inna, "others love and then forget,
Mine like a weight in my bosom lies,
Mine ever with memory's tears is wet,
Why is it that my love never dies?"

A cloudless day, a season of inviting weather,
  Inna had partially regained her health,
She and Lord Chancey Douglass stood on deck together,
  Viewing the day's splendor and golden wealth.

.They heard a step and a voice say "step with care,"
  They turned and saw it might have been an angel's form,
An angel's face so saint-like fair,
  Indicative of no inward storm,
  An invalid leaning on her father's arm,
A childish face and figure to charm at once the eye,
And Inna saw with joy, rather than alarm,
  A look from Douglass follow as she glided by.

The spell that *incident* and *idle fancy* had created
  Was broken, but to be more firm,
And if by that fancy-wrought attachment he was elated,
  Behold him the true love lesson learn ;
Clara Landon was a Southern belle,
And being in Inna's confidence firmly now,
  One day told *her* romance ; Clara knew Osgood well,
  She said with a soft blush on 'her brow.

Then into Inna's listening, willing ears,
  She poured the story of his college days,
His laborious study, doubts and fears,
  His thousand and one peculiar ways;
The excitement and commotion of his leaving home,
  Floating rumors that he'd run away insane,
The flying reports that back to them had come
  Of his resolving health and love to gain.

"Inna," said she, "if it's he on whom you've bestowed your heart,
　You may know he's worthy in everyway;
The Southern girls would all with friends and fortune part
　If 'twould win Clarence Osgood's love to-day;"
There was one girl I fancied he liked once,
　'Twas Alice Lorraine, your brother's wife,
But I declared myself a presuming dunce,
　When he vowed he'd *never* have a *wife.*

"And, oh, Inna, I could easily have loved him, too,
　But on me he'd not even bestow a smile;
So I soon learned it wouldn't do
　To fall in love with one so misanthropic the while.
Now, *ma belle*, Inna, I'm *content* if you are,
　But if you've gained ascendency to *his* heart
You may consider yourself a special favored star,
　Who's won the *prize* in Love's expansive mart."

Days passed on, they reached the other side,
　Time flew in love's sweet mysterious style,
Till the happy lord and victor with his charming bride,
　Filed one morn up fair St. Maria's isle.
Then with lovely Inna in their care
　They started for America's praiseworthy land,
And Inna smiled, for now she knew her lover's name was fair,
　That his had *never* been a murderer's hand.

She thought of the many a happy hour to come
　When she'd tease him about the plot he played;
And pictures of her trans-Atlantic home
　In the chamber of her mind were laid.

"Oh," tho't she, "that he should assume a blight on his fair name,
  To gain a love unbiased, undying, true;
But on myself I can cast no blame—
  My darling, I've been true to you.

     *   *   *   *   *   *

On the shore of Lake Michigan sits a woman still fair,
  And still with a pure and youthful brow,
Yet a pensive shadow is lingering there,
  Leaving no room for joy's bright glow;
Little Clarence, a child of four, plays merrily at her side,
  Wondering the while at her flowing tears,
While she mournfully watches the tide,
  And thinks, "Oh, the gloomy years!"

"Ten years ago on this spot we met,
  I found him here with his head lying low;
Oh, my lost darling, shall I ever forget—
  Forget *thee*, or *that night*, oh, no!
Three years since I watched thy parting breath,
  And knew thy promising life was done;
True to thee ever in life and in death,
  And for thee I'll haunt the shore of Lake Michigan.

NEVER DESPAIR.

FROM " FORGET-ME-NOT."

IF your pathway be not smooth,
  And your future look not fair,
Or you get vexed at some little trifle,
  Oh, don't give up in despair.

Brighter days will come to you,
  Days that will be fair,
If you only will have courage,
  And not give up in despair.

Though dark and dreary be your lot,
  And fortune frown on you to-day;
To-morrow your luck may change,
  And fortune turn the other way.

Never despair, let come what will,
  Think there are brighter days in store;
Press on, press on with courage bold
  And never despair any more.

AN INVENTORY.

FROM " FORGET-ME-NOT."

A ROUGH, bare and broken floor,
One hinge off the only door,
A rusty stove, minus one leg,
A worn out cap on a broken peg,
Old hats and caps for window lights,
(They'll keep out storm on stormy nights),
Three old and broken plates,
A cup, and two saucers that are not mates,
One iron spoon, and part of another,
A tea-pot minus handle and cover,
An old kettle, with many a crack,
Two old spiders that handles lack,
A rusty, worn out can,
One bottomless basin, and old tin pan,
Parts of a few knives and forks,
A jug, and a stack of corks,
A table minus a leaf and leg,
The top and sides of a liquor keg;
A woman crouching in perfect awe,
Near a poor old pallet of straw,
On which a haggard man lies,
Uttering wild and piercing cries;
Six hungry mouths that will not be shut,
Is an inventory of a drunkard's hut.

SINGLE THE GOLDEN THREAD.

There is a curtain filmy, and a trifle slender,
    That screens the chamber of the past;
All dreams bright, or dark, harsh or tender
    Are within, in its portals cast;
And memory doth this curtain lift,
    To show us many a tangled web;
But as the bright and dark we sift,
    Let's single the golden thread.

As we journey o'er the waves of the Sea of Life,
    We meet its turbulent ups and downs,
But as we battle with its avalanche of strife,
    Behold a smile amid the frowns.
Life is full we know of roughest thorns,
    And bitter, oft, its briny cup;
But let us remember the few sunny morns
    That light our pathway up.

City of the beauteous South, so fair,
    To thy arms I gladly came,
With many a castle reared in air,
    Of the sunbeams to be at my disposal lain,
Lo, the airy structure fell—the rain poured down,
    But though my heart sank down like lead,
As I beheld the element's dark frown,
    I singled at once the golden thread.

What is life? one vast sea of trouble,
  Prosperity? something that few may hold.
And wealth? a shining, fickle bubble,
  That leads to the selfish love of gold;
But it's neither wealth nor station's pass,
  That's to make us paths of joy tread,
But simply from Life's chaotic mass,
  To single the golden thread.

COLUMBIA, S. C., April 1, 1874.

"SOMETIME."

AH, that treasured word *sometime*, ah, the joyful song,
  That it merrily warbles down in, the heart,
While delicious memories cluster and throng,
  Up from the past, causing tears to start:
Girlish tears, perchance, as the school anniversary nears,
And they must part, who've been friends for years.
  They part with many an arranged prospective plan,
  And promises of a future meeting chime,
To meet again in the ranks of life's great van,
  To meet in that beauteous, far off *sometime*.

Sweet little treasured *sometime* fills the heart with joy's boon,
  As do the matins of birds, when summer gay
Springs from the arms of sullen winter's gloom,
  And on snow-capped mountains is born rosy day.

At last, if life's thousand meandering streams
Should never float us nearer earthly dreams,
  The woven wreaths of hope that perish,
  And vanish in this unpitying clime,
Air-castle dreams we so fondly cherish,
  May be realized 'mong eternal hills of a celestial *some-
  time.*

OLD YEAR, GOOD-BYE.

AH, Old Year, and must I part with thee,
Must say farewell to seventy-three?
  Ah, Old Year, 'tis with many a tear,
For I've found thee true and certain ;
And what behind the Future's curtain
  May for me be lurking near?
Ah, thou hast brought me joy,
Which another year may all destroy,
And my brightest hopes belie—
Old Year, and *must* I say good-bye?

Ah' I'm with thee in thy last hour,
Recalling the many a sunny bower
  In which thou hast led with gentle tread !
Ah, Old Year, my friend, I shall forget thee not,
Thou cam'st with me to this fair spot,
  And here I must leave thee dead.

When I return to my Northern valley fair,
Old Year thou'lt not go with me there;
Afar from my native home I see thee die,
Old Year, and *must* say good-bye?

Is it strange that I am sighing, Old Year, to see thee dying,
    While distance lies between
    Me and one familiar scene?
Ah, Old Year, I ask thee still to linger near,
Friend so true and kind, stay a bit and help me find
    Some within this far-off clime,
    Whose friendship may equal thine.
Thy mission's done, and beneath this Southern sky,
I whisper thee, Old Year, good-bye.

WILMINGTON, N. C., December 31, 1873.

LOVE GOES AFOOT.

LUCY GRAY is a favorite, she is young and fair,
She is the petted and only daughter of a millionaire;
And lo, on the instant when her slightest wish is made,
As though 'twere a sovereign's it is quickly obeyed;
Seemingly she háth everything heart could desire,
Interests of which she ne'er might weary or tire,
But listen! while she sits at the lattice with closed eyes,
Up through the shutter float deep-drawn sighs.

Lucy has suitors who are both gay and grave,
Some timid and weak, others valiant and brave;
But she turns from all smiles courteous and bland,
Regretting her father's broad acres and extensive wide land.
As strange a tale you think as ever was told,
That Lucy is sorry for father's bright gold,
Yet she out of her window oft looks with a sigh,
For one lone thing that money can't buy.

Fair Lucy tosses back each saucy curl,
Wishing anon she were but a poor man's girl;
She is troubled at table, and troubled in bed
She worries and frets her poor little head,
And, tearfully, to papa, she's oft heard to say,
"Oh, to know who loves your wealth, and *who* Lucy Gray!"
And her papa smiling says to himself,
"I'll try and find out for the dear little elf."

And one day thro' the air the startling news sailed,
The old millionaire—the banker has failed;
And Lucy soon found by words formal and cold
That she was lov'd less than her father's vast gold.
"But," said she, "tho' of my fortune I am bereft,
'Twere best to know the real friends I have left."
But only *one* entered the low cottage door
Who cared not that Lucy was poor.

And when their fortune flew back one auspicious day
Many a fair glance was directed that way;
And many sought the maiden to greet,
Who had passed her coldly in the street.

Turning from a score of suitors wealthy and bland,
Waiving them back with motion of hand,
" Riches may ride in a carriage gilded and gay,
But love goes afoot," murmurs fair Lucy Gray.

MEMORIAL DAY.

*To Mrs. Johnson, and the other ladies of Atlanta, who have
contributed to the efforts of the day, these simple lines are dedicated.*

BLESSED day, singled from the rest,
    By memory's pure test,
To wreathe the soldier's graves !
    Strew floral gifts where they lie,
    For surely God's eye
Looks down upon you who kindly and true;
    Remember your country's braves;
May Memory's laurels fondly enclose
Graves where the lov'd ones calmly repose :
    On this beauteous sunny soil,
    Where many a Southern gem doth coil
Round that fair memorial spot, the noble soldier's burying lot,
Where the Southern sunbeams shine,
You, these floral tokens twine :
Wreathe with a tender thought and with a tear,
The graves of those so loved and dear.

ATLANTA, GA., April 30, 1874.

TO MY COUSIN ON HIS FIFTEENTH BIRTHDAY.

THE winter months are o'er, and March again is here,
  And though many a rambling tho't it bring,
I know that you, my cousin, complete your fifteenth year,
  On this first day of smiling Spring;
And mid the varied objects that claim my whole attention,
  On which, perhaps my mind should dwell,
Memory fain at this time would mention,
  One far away, I love so well.
She wanders to you, lov'd one, awhile,
  Though roving beneath this sunny clime,
Fancy leaps o'er the many a weary mile,
  To press my lips to thine.
Dear coz., enshrined in Friendship's circling arms,
  With a tho't of our many bright spent hours,
Love sends you through imagination's charms,
  A gem from these Southern bowers.

Dear cousin, lov'd playmate of days gone by,
  Still prized friend of my affection,
I'm far to-day from thy cold Northern sky,
  My path of life in an opposite direction:
Where flowers bloom the whole year long,
  Where the magnolia and orange blossoms wave,
And the warblers constantly pour forth their song
  And golden hues the bright sky bathe—

Here where hath dwelt quarrel and contention,
  Here where many a gallant form once fell,
I sit to-day, lov'd one, and my attention
  Is led o'er mountain steep and flowery dell—
Away from this memorable Southern spot to-day,
  To climb with thee that gentle hill-slope,
Fancies, how swift they fly! nor do I bid them stay—
  Not from thee, sweet cousin, of many a cherished hope.

ELIZABETHTOWN, N. C., March 1, 1874.

OVER THE WAY.

OVER the way bright lamps are burning,
And dainty fingers the music turning,
    Over the way, over the way.
The house is filled with warmth and light,
And everything seems cheerful and bright
    Over the way, over the way.

Over the way light feet are tripping,
And through the Lanciers are gayly skipping,
    Over the way, over the way.
Loved ones are fondly lingering near,
All lonely moments to kindly cheer,
    Over the way, over the way.

Over the way is drinking and feasting,
And blithe the hearts that there are beating,
   Over the way, over the way;
And some are lingering near to prize
The gentle look from drooping eyes
   Over the way, over the way.

Oh, surely there can be naught to alloy,
Or e'en to mar their peace, happiness and joy,
   Over the way, over the way.
Oh, can there be an entrance of gloom
In that gorgeously decorated room,
   Over the way, over the way.

Ah, my friend, 'twill be no sin,
Come with me and I'll usher you in,
   Over the way, over the way.
See *her* standing near that floral stand,
Her head reclining on her hand,
   Over the way, over the way.

Blinding tears now dim the sight
Of those eyes, a moment ago so bright,
   Over the way, over the way—
Alas! alas! there's deep sorrow there,
Tho' the external seemed so fair,
   Over the way, over the way.

And thus it is where'er we go,
All have trouble we may not know,
 Over the way, over the way.
We should be content with our own lot,
Whether it be in mansion or cot,
And never sigh for what *seems* gay,
 Over the way, over the way.

RESIGNATION.

A will, oh! Father, submissive to Thine,
Though many a wish we have to resign,
On the platform that Ambition can make,
When, lo, we see the platform break!
Of course we cannot tell the reason why,
For it seemed firm to our earthly eye;
But that eye that watches o'er wrecks of Time
Is clearer far than yours and mine,
That o'er our lives a vigil keeps,
An eye, an eye that never sleeps!

And can we not the power find
To make our will to His resigned?
It may come hard to some at first,
Who for Life's painted baubles thirst,
For every emergency we must be prepared
To drop, if needful, pleasures shared,

For choicest idols shattered may lie
Broken fragments before the eye,
And many a dream gilded brightly o'er
May vanish our very gaze before ;
And many a gem we think to grasp
Perish e'en within our clasp ;
But, oh, to say : Thy grace impart,
Thy will, oh, God, within my heart !

TO GEORGIA AND KATIE MARSH.

My friends, we part, and what can I, what shall I say
Just now, that were not as pieces of broken clay ?

How sternly Friendship points to a tower of her erection,
To the warm place you've gained in my affection !

A spot that shall be neither unfading nor small,
Remains, henceforth, for you in Memory's hall !

Health, friends, and fortune now smile on you,
But should there come a time they'd prove untrue,

Love and gratitude unbroken need no mend,
In your Northern guest *then* find a friend.

A stranger far from her Northern valley fair
Had come to breathe your Southern air ;

And among the warm hearts the South doth hold,
Hath found two unfading gems of gold!

This rare gift, culled from your floral bowers,
Will oft remind me of these happy hours!

I shall ne'er forget you on Life's treacherous sea,
And, oh, my friends, do you oft remember me?

But, hark! the engine shrieks, the parting moment's nigh,
Star friends of the sunny South, good-bye!

Here we met to part, and part to meet, perhaps *no* more
But Faith points to a bright, reunion Shore!

AUGUSTA, Ga.

ONLY JESSIE.

(INCIDENTAL.)

"Who is she, sister, that young girl,
    Lovely, yet with a sad expression on her face,
Dark eyes and hair and tangled curl,
    And more, such a sweet and winning grace!
I met her on the stairs—there is a charm about her—
    Her cheeks with modest blushes glowing!"
"Why," said Florence, "so much talk about her?
    It's only Jessie, the girl who does our sewing."

"Only Jessie," murmured Captain Wilbur Lee,
  "And she must drudge from 'morn till dewy eve,'
No sympathy for 'only Jessie'—we will see,
  Here Fate may a web of romance weave ;
Ha, ha, Florence and Blanche, how they would scold
  Did they *dream* such a tho't were in my head ;
But I never cared for fashion or shining gold,
  And begged a path of Love to tread."

On Blank street there's a happy home to-day,
  Two contented hearts and no repining—
Two sunny lives ever blithe and gay,
  Seeing to every cloud a silver lining.
Around, the blossoms of peace twine a garland fair,
  And the rippling murmur of Love doth glide ;
Captain Wilbur Lee dwells there,
  With "only Jessie" by his side.

COMMENCEMENT DAY.

THE moments fly ! I lay my book aside,
  For Fancy travels o'er miles that lie between ;
How swift, how swift, oh, thoughts, ye glide
  To that bright, eventful scene !
Read ! study ! not in this sacred bit of time,
  For, hark ! the clock strikes one,
And by the letters I've counted in a line,
  That oration already has begun.

Childish, weak, perhaps you say,
　　'Twere weaker still to let memory slumber,
And forget, on this anniversary day,
　　The brightest Star of all the number—
The brightest, *then*, the brightest *now*,
　　Perhaps I've reason for praise so strong?
None, but to twine laurels o'er the brow,
　　Where Conscience tells that they belong.

Memory, Memory, thy trust still keep,
　　That sonorous voice rises clear,
Then falls with a cadence thrilling, deep—
　　Memory, Memory, linger near.
Fain at his feet I'd lay a floral gift,
　　But Fate decreed it should not be;
But, oh, Memory, thy filmy curtain uplift,
　　And do thy duty well for me!

Waft to him o'er gentle Fancy's wing
　　My wishes for him this hour;
A substitute for the gift I'd bring,
　　From the choicest floral bower;
For in this distant Western clime to-day
　　A prayer for him arises now,
That many a laurel and bright bay
　　May twine o'er that noble brow.

THE AGE OF SCANDAL.

WE'VE had the age of iron, age of silver and age of gold,
  An many etceteras we could name,   .
And now we have the age of scandal unblushingly bold,
  The age of scandal and of shame.

Why does a dark cloud hang o'er the world to-day?
  Threatening the downfall of earth's great guide,
And, lo, as we from this great sorrow turn away,
  Minor shadows of the kind we see on every side.

Fierce tempests are impending life's frail barge,
  And we gaze at the boisterous elements with pity.
While one storm-cloud hangs o'er the world at large,
  Smaller ones environ each town and city.

Jersey City and Canada, one place is no safer than the rest,
  We ask that Fate may so the tongue of slander handle,
As to divert such clouds from this Garden of the West;
  For we live in a net-work wove in the Age of Scandal.

CHICAGO, Aug. 27, 1874.   ı

VALLEY OF THE ORISKANY.

VALLEY of Learning! I'll not forget thee now,
  Valley that I've oft and e'er admired!
For in thy portals Fate twined o'er my brow,
  All that has e'er my poor pen inspired.
The poetic muse first met me in thy inviting arms,
Delightful nook, I'd not deny thy charms.

Yet I think of thee as a gem off which the gilding has been
    swept,
  I lov'd thee once, think kindly of thee still,
In a corner of my heart thy picture's kept;
  But thy allurements for me have lost their thrill,
Ah, Valley of the Oriskany, model for an artist's eye,
Thou could'st hardly lure me from haunts beneath this western
    sky!

FATAL FRIENDSHIP.

The title of the following poem is taken from a Journal article entitled "Fatal Friendship," and referring to the scandal topic of the day.

FRIENDSHIP warms our hearts as sunshine warms the flowers,
　Refreshes us just as rain revives the grass.
Friendship is a fair shrub in this cold world of ours,
　But there is a limit o'er which *none* should pass.
Prize that Friendship that gets of Purity its birthright natal,
But beware that *friendship* known as *fatal*.

Friendship of innate goodness of mind, heart and soul,
　From the deep well-spring of virtue born,
Such should we place on Friendship's roll,
　And from all other turn with scorn.

Pure and wholesome friendship we would cherish,
　Words and tho'ts connected in a kindly link,
A closer friendship! let e'en the base tho't perish,
　'Tis a dangerous and polluted brink.

A closer friendship, the very thought we *hate*!
　Nothing were friendship that were not pure ;
Friendship is to refine the character and elevate,
　And not the curse of hell procure.

When friendly word and acts have turned to guile,
  Then friendship has turned to gall,
Stamp on it with a scornful, bitter smile,
  Ere you let it make you fall.

What is friendship, we beg and seek to know ?
  Something to do good and help one up,
And not with honeyed words of flattery seek one's woe,
  Through Satan's sin-filled cup !

Sympathy ! perchance the world may blame,
  But for those who step on shallow friendship's ground,
And through its vestibule are brought to shame,
  There's no sympathy or patience to be found.

Spurn one who on the plea of friendship's chaste relation,
  Steps through decorum's closéd gate ;
Love one who'd steal a *priceless* reputation ?
  Be the burden of the song to *hate.*

Who'd trust a heart with that unstable creature,
  Who's dignity lies in Impropriety's chaotic mass,
Push him back for one who has virtue's feature,
  Who *minds* the *limit* of friendship none should pass.
We invite Friendship that from purity has its birthright natal,
But *abhor* a friendship known as *fatal.*

RESPONSIVE LINES.

ON RECEIVING AN EULOGY ON "FORGET-ME-NOT."

MANY long months may have rolled away,
  Cloaking a mystery behind their curtain,
That mysteries will come to light some day,
  Is *possible*, yea, almost *certain;*
Though mountains and rivers may intervene,
  Twixt the mystery discovered and mystery unraveled,
And she who carried the mythical dream,
  O'er long miles have traveled,
Yet in due time the obscured cometh to light,
And the hidden link is brought into sight.

Ah, it may have seemed locked in portals on high,
  Safe from we mortals of earth,
Free and secure from every eye,
  Only one knows its origin, one knows its birth,
So sure there's never a fear nor a doubt—
  "She can't know the author of the lines I send—"
But lo, a day when the truth comes out,
  My modest, respected friend,
The mystery's author I've seen ; hence gratitude o'ertwines,
And stamps her signal 'mid the friendly lines.

My grateful and heartfelt thanks let me now return,
  For those delicate eulogistic lines,
For the sentiment so kindly in its turn
  Bestowed on my inexperienced rhymes.

From many a lip I've heard fair eulogies start,
   To rest on the childish tho'ts there told,
While many have given them in their heart,
   A warm spot e'er to hold ;
But one hath penned what lips could not tell,
Fairest praise from Modesty's pure well.

And doth my feeble rhymes contain " a charm ?"
   May God make them more and more,
And do they " console mid life's alarms "
   And on her turbulent shore?
Have they painted " landscapes in castle dreams,"
   Held one " fancy to inspire,"
May the fairy muse still search for scenes,
   To tune her crippled lyre :
Do the simple thoughts o'er my first effort's page,
Lead one back to realms of "boyhood's age ?"

A voice than others clearer, firmer, more sublime,
   Rises oft on imagination's wing,
And through the filmy mists of gathering time,
   Will its clarion accents ring :
That voice, and the hand that penned those lines,
   Must in fancy be linked together,
Both from Intellect's deepest mines,
   O'er Progress' rolling river.
Words and writing marked by one true would not bear blame,
Surely their resource must be the same.

Poems not from a standard author's pen,
"Inspiring" you generously call,
And give them with the author then,
A place in Memory's hall ;
Well, she is grateful to the mystic Nymph of Fate,
Who explored the mystery's ranks,
And pointed to the one though late,
Who merits and receives alike her thanks.
Accept the lines that lame Poesy deigns to lend,
With the kindly wishes of "a friend."

BOSTON, August, 1873.

DARK HOURS.

OH, the hours may be dark, my friend,
But I ask you not to despair,
For Providence in time will surely send
A path for you more fair.
Black as night may be the hours,
Instead of fainting, work and pray,
And soon bright sunny flowers,
Will bloom along your way ;
You need not accuse me now of preaching,
One thing to talk, another to do,
Were it not for experience's bitter teaching,
This book were not before you.

Just as blank despair by me did stand,
    With her tempting voice to urge,
God reached out His own right hand,
    And drew me from her verge.

SALUTATORY POEMS.

COMPOSED FOR A READING IN THE SOUTH.

MY friends, while you this evening come from homes so warm
        and bright,
    And know the gentle Southern breeze that blows,
I meet you a stranger here to-night,
    As the day sinketh into calm repose :
Yes, I've come from yonder Northern valley fair,
    Where many a cherished memory lies,
That I may the healthful breezes share,
    Beneath your sunny, Southern skies;
That I within these walls some friends may find,
    Is there a doubt or danger?
Oh, will the hand of friendship, kind,
    Welcome the Northern stranger?
Ah, I'm far to-night from scenes and friends so dear,
You'll not refuse a smile the stranger's heart to cheer.

It is with feelings that rise from the well-springs of emotion,
  That before you I now appear,
That aside from the noisy world's commotion
  For a while I meet you here.
But from the many thot's that to our minds may cluster.
  May but pleasant ones be singled,
May we here forget life's fantastic bluster,
  As though in it we had not mingled :
Let's every misty shadow far from us cast,
  Knowing God doth all things well.
Come, dove of Peace, dispel the shadows of the past,
  Henceforth with us to dwell,
And as thro' gratitude's dewy tear we greet this shining star,
May no cloud the beauteous vision mar.

Ah, ye winning South, which Fancy hath painted many a time,
  With thy brilliant and extensive charms
Glowing like the sparkles of ruby wine,
  Within thy fair, encircling arms !
Beautiful are my Northern scenes and fine,
  And some 'twere sad to leave,
But o'er the beauties of this mild and genial clime,
  Friendship must her laurels weave ;
I've left haunts watered by affection's showers,
  Yet says Justice's e'er impartial mouth,
Thou'st found a recompense within the bowers,
  Of the radiant, sunny South ;
Henceforth the smiling South will hold a spot,
Too bright in Memory to be forgot.

As onward sweepeth the ceaseless river of Time,
  There'll be a picture on Memory's page,
That will brighter and still brighter shine,
  When these eyes are dimmed by age ;
That picture round which pleasant thoughts will e'er abound,
  Spotless pure and all untainted,
Will be my first reception on your ground,
  In brightest colors painted ;
Ah, inviting South, thy embrace is large and wide,
  Thy welcome frank and free,
And thou'st now a stranger to thy side,
  Whose good wishes are for thee ;
May Prosperity shed o'er thee her brightest flowers
And Peace e'er dwell within thy charming bowers.

THE OLD OAK TREE.

AH, yes, 'tis standing firmly as ever,
  Tho' twenty years have slipped away,
Since we three boys sat together,
  Under its shade that Autumn day ;
Three of us young and void of care,
  Already yearning to win young Fame
And building castles in the air,
  Each carved on the Oak his name.

I see it again! but lo, remorseless Time
  Has borne changes on his wing,
Leaving of those three names, but mine,
  A picture of that happy day to bring;
And of the other two you wish me tell?
  'Neath the cruel sea one has his bed,
The other at distant Vicksburg fell,
  And there they found him dead.

"Ah," said Ben, on that memorable day,
  Just twenty years gone by,
"Across the Ocean, fleet and gay
  My ships shall meet the eye."
Said Ned: "I'll be a hero in my time,"
  And his cheek flushed as he spoke;
But there remaineth now but mine,
  Of the names carved on the Oak.

THE LOST PHOTOGRAPH.

Gone! the little miniature I've treasured so long,
  Rudely torn from its resting place,
Who else can prize the smile and the song
  That clustered around that face?
Gone! yet from memory it shall not depart,
'Tis firmly engraven on the tablets of heart.

Gone ! and is it weakness now to shed tears
  O'er that prized gem of art ?
Cherished picture that love alone endears,'
  Live in the precincts of my heart :
Yea, live for aye in Memory's fond clasp,
Picture oft hugged by affection's warm grasp.

"My darling girl," "my dear little pet,"
  And I repose in thy arms once more;
And, friend, dearest but *one*, I see-thee yet,
  'Smiles lingering thy loved face o'er.
Ah, papa, dear papa, with grief I'm near wild,
They've taken thy picture, so dear to thy child.

I feel ready to die, yet must I live,
  And let go the treasure I've pressed ;
Much else is gone, greater in value yet more would I give
  For *that* than all of the rest :
Wicked hands robbed me of that prized little gem,
Methinks dark shadows ever must haunt them.

CHICAGO, August 1, 1874.

DEATH OF LINA MILLER.

LOVELY LINA, child of promise, bright and fair,
  While thy gentle form we e'er shall miss,
From this misty world of grief and care,
  Thou hast entered eternal bliss.

Ah, yes, when we look on the pains of thy brief years,
  Thy meek and patient mien,
We quickly quell all doubts and fears—
  No shadow comes between.

No shadow, Lina, dear, our hopes to mar,
  In the gem-like home beyond the sky,
We see thee, saint-like, angelic star
  Of the angel's choir on High.

Life's road is mountainous and hard to tread,
  Its hills are rough and steep ;
But thou, loved one, wilt no more tread
  Its abysses, dark and deep.

Lovely Lina, child of broad affection,
  So young, amiable, good and pure,
How could we let thee go but to His protection
  That will for aye endure ?

But God's promise floats upon our ears,
  We have lain thee in his arms,
To hold thee e'er from grief and fears,
  And free from life's alarms.

And when we've walked this dismal road,
  Till its burdens all are o'er,
May we, when we drop its heavy load,
  Meet again to part no more.

AN ARGUMENT ON FIRST LOVE.

AFFIRMATIVE BY F. R. HAFLAND.

THE gem you'd win for aye to rest,
Upon your warm, your loyal breast—
Though her charms excel every other,
She must never have loved another;
Nay, not only that you ask, but more,
Not only must she ne'er have loved before,
But not a feeling from Affection's well,
In its ever-flowing, curving bend,
Must have been bestowed on a former friend;
And still, again, you'd have her tell,
With a first-love accented tone of voice
That you are her *first*, her *only* choice
Excuse me if the liberty I take
To accuse you of a slight mistake;
Yet dictating Conscience assures
That opinions differ widely,
The argument we will settle mildly—
Allow me my opinion, I leave you yours.

Remote from cities gay a maiden lived
    Within a sylvan dell,
Of fashion's votaries she knew but little
    And drank from Nature's well;

Artless and graceful she had grown,
But suitors alas she'd none;
In fact the number was small who knew her,
Her intimate associates were fewer.

To that glen, tired of city airs and graces,
    A wealthy stranger came;
His was the manliest of faces,
    He bore an honored name;
And in this rustic, woodland glade,
He woes the simple, trusting maid.

She loved him, for she knew no other,
    But e'er three years glided by
She bestowed her love upon another,
    Who chanced to charm her eye.
He'd said: " If e'er I form *that* connection
I must be the first of *her* affection."

Another who had won many lovers,
    At last on one let her true love rest—
" I love you," said she, " above all others,
    If not my *first* love, e'er my best;"
And who with so mature a love would part,
Tho' childish fancies had dwelt within the heart?

MORAL.

SEEK not the rose o'er which bushes twine,
    Concealing it from the eye,
But that which hangs on the visible vine,
    Nodding to passers-by;

That hath diffused its perfume perhaps upon many
  But remaineth unyielding yet;
For difficult to be plucked by any,
  Surely a prize to get—
The rose that so many have tried to gain,
  Then have had to let fall,
They have tried, and tried in vain,
  It yieldeth to you above them all :
Think not its brightest perfume wasted
  If some have imbibed its sweetness,
They have never won, have never tasted,
  What gives your life completeness :
Sympathy may have caused it with some smiles to part,
  To brighten another's view,
But that gem of all—the faithful heart—
  Remaineth true to you.

READY TO GO.

"I'LL be all ready, you see, to go,"
And her bright eyes were all aglow ;
"When papa comes he'll be in a hurry,
Then, you see, he won't have to worry ;
And papa never likes us to be late,
This time I'll not make him wait ;
Better be ready and not to go,
Than go and not be ready, you know."

But the hours went slowly by,
And papa came not nigh :
Bright spots tinged the tiny cheek,
And in less than one short week
A messenger came in at the door,
Glided swiftly across the floor,
And bore the darling of that home away
Into one long, unending day.
One sweet tho't came as they laid her low,
Their lovely idol was *ready to go.*

LINES TO THE OLD YEAR.

OLD year, thy weeks and months have fled away,
Many a sunny hour and golden day,
Mingled with shadows by the way,
   Yet now we heave a sigh :
Many a blessing thou hast brought,
With happiness and wisdom fraught,
Many a lesson hast thou taught,
   But now, old year, good bye !

Oft the marriage bells have rung,
Alike the funeral songs been sung,
And Time his harpstrings oft has strung,
   His sacred duty to not belie ;

Thou'st brought joys too bright to last,
And some with shadows overcast,
But thy work is in the chamber of the Past.
Old Year, Old Year, good bye!

IN MEMORY OF GEORGE E. ARCHER.

George E. Archer was a member of the Y. M. C. Association of Chicago, to which, and his friends, these lines are respectfnlly inscribed.

WE this slight poetic tribute bring as a memorial token,
For again we behold the Association number broken;
Yea, Death again with cold unyielding hand,
Hath left a vacant seat within this golden band,
And now as from time to time we gather here,
And miss the voice so wont to greet our ear,
And see that familiar form no more,
And know 'twill never enter the Lyceum door,
At the reunion hour may Memory gently stand,
Tenderly recalling this bright star of the band.

Gone to those bright realms where no sorrow enters,
But fondest tho't around thy memory centers;
Thou'st joined that choir where melodious anthems clear,
Are ringing sweetly throughout an endless year,
Free from the boisterous waves of sin and strife,
Ended thus early the contest in thy Battle of Life.

There storm-clouds of trouble burst not around,
And the genuine spirit of peace doth abound,
While here we mourn over the loss of our band,
There's rejoicing on that shining strand.

Gone, ana we know thy earthly work is done,
Yet thy hand was ever a helping one,
And long on Life's changeful, uncertain sea,
Will the Association cherish memories of thee;
And 'tis a comfort now to each stricken heart,
To know that thou acted so goodly a part.
We behold marks of good works on every side,
While with us thou stemmed Life's varying tide,
Traces of good deeds are not obliterated by time's sands,
They're woven in memory's encircling bands.

The Lyceum meets the same, yet not the same,
For it crosses from its record one endearing name,
Blotted from our earthly, joined unto another,
A record pure enrolls the name of our departed brother,
That list bears the names of those who've gone to rest,
Of those who've passed life's trial test.
Gone from our midst, we close our tribute with a sigh,
Brother of our affection we bid thee now good-bye;
And when life with its " ups and downs" is o'er,
May the Association meet on that farther shore.

THE BROKEN PROMISE.

FAR from his Southern home, Harry Bowden came,
    To the embrace of a beauteous Northern glen,
To the walls of an Alma Mater of undying fame,
    That had sent forth authors, orators and statesmen ;
And in that work that Art and Nature smiled on,
    While storing his head with useful knowledge,
He learned a lesson easier far to con,
    Than any he found in college.

The words were easy, " my pet," " dear," and " dove,"
    The text-book easy throughout to learn,
The oft-repeated words of never-fading love,
    Held in Fate's romantic urn ;
The object of his affection was fair Lucy Blish,
    He was rich, and she was poor, 'tis true,
But a prettier sight to see one could not wish,
    For love o'er them his fairest mantel threw.

Lucy was a widow's child ; their only dower
    Was a spot of ground and cottage home,
Lucy knew little of fashion, being Nature's modest flower.
    And Nature by her had justice done ;
To her youthful eyes unused to fashion seeing,
    Her Southern lover, with his brave, ancestral name,
Was a great and glorious being,
    In whose keeping her first fond love she'd lain.

Time flew! how rapidly to these two lovers!
　All too swift and gay to tell;
What a volume of joy or sorrow a small space covers,
　And Harry bid his college home farewell!
They parted with many a token lòve bedew'd,
　With many a promise that naught should sever,
With many a glowing description strewed,
　Of love that should live forever.

Harry returned to his own proud sunny soil,
　Where mother and sister, with arrow pointed,
Aimed his fair love dreams to foil;
　It took effect, and lo, disjointed,
The love four years had wove together—
　He could not endure the tempest's hover—
A year sped by—a farewell letter,
　He loved her still—but all was over.

Lucy's mother died—the cottage house was sold,
　The scanty avails were hugged with care,
As the miser doats o'er his hoarded gold,
　Did Lucy doat o'er her treasured share;
Love, with friends and fortune was resigned,
　If not, 'twas carefully 'mong by-gones lain,
Henceforth, the culture of her mind,
　Was to be her sole objective aim.

*　　*　　*　　*　　*　　*

Five years have joined the gone-by ones,
  The bells of Charleston a merry peal are ringing,
Through the magnolia grove a wedding group now comes,
  While gay voices a marriage tune are singing,
For Harry Bowden bestows his hand, not heart, to-day,
  On one whom fortune hath richly blest,
The haughty heiress, dark-eyed Edith May,
  His mother's choice from all the rest.

And among the many belles assembled there,
  Was one the cynosure of all eyes,
Not only was she youthful, wealthy, beloved and fair,
  But the brilliant author of "Sunny Skies;"
And the low murmured words "she's here,"
  Sounded through the densely crowded room,
That name fell on Harry Bowden's ear,
  As an omen of future gloom.

      *   *   *   *   *   *

Long Branch! and they met again on that fair spot,
  After five years more had fled,
He'd been true to Edith, though sorrow had been his lot,
  For 'twas a wild, unloving life she led.
Two years before, she died, and now his intense wish,
  While anew his never-forgotten love was burning,
Was to gain again the love of Lucy Blish,
  Was her old affection, too, returning?

The night was calm and breezy, the air was soft and delicious,
    The spot all that one could wish,
The moon-lit hour was surely propitious,
    But oh, world-renowned and stately Lucy Blish !
Did passionate words of love so eloquently arranged,
    E'er fall on such deaf ears ? ah, never !
Said she, and the passive face remained unchanged,
    "Your promise broken, was broken *forever.*"

A LEGACY.

PERCHANCE you are despondent, with weariness cast down,
    Because you haven't wealth and fame,
But oh, dispel at once that quickly gathering frown,
    If you've still your spotless name ;
A legacy more priceless far than gold,
A legacy whose value is untold.
Avalanches of trouble may roll around,
    But there'll be a path to lead you out some way,
If only you step on the firm, hard ground,
    And not where it's ready to sink with foul decay ;
But whatever your loss, whatever your gain,
Hug like a miser your spotless name.
Oh, sink not down, or turn from the world with dread,
    If this golden legacy still remain,
Though stormy and rough the paths you tread,
    Part not with your spotless name ;
When friends and fortune vanish on swift flying wings,
This legacy'll stand 'mong imperishable things.

ON THE DEATH OF MRS. CHARLOTTE A. BARTLETT.

Charlotte A. Bartlett, wife of Rev. William Bartlett, pastor of Plymouth Church, and daughter of Walter P. Flanders of Milwaukee, died at Berne, Switzerland, Sat., Sept. 12th, of heart disease.

SWEET sister, so loved and so dear, thy smile and kind words of
    cheer
  With thy spirit have vanished away.
So lovely and pure in heart, 'tis hard, sweet sister, to part;
  But this world was too cold for thee to stay:
Deeply we mourn thee now, with thy pure gentle brow,
  And know here we shall see thee no more.
Far o'er the watery deep, sister, thou wentest to sleep,
  To awake on a starry-lit shore.

Across the storm-tossed ocean, with its ceaseless, incessant mo-
    tion,
  Thy life-work, sweet sister, was ended.
Over the waves of the ocean of life, were lulled from all strife,
  And with quiet and peacefulness blended;
Toward all goodness thy heart yearned, and thy crown immortal
    is earned.
  Rest in those fair celestial realms;
While deeply we mourn thee here, and cherish thy memory dear,
  In a world that dim care overwhelms.

There's a sadness in the Life Boat to-day, as thy sweet spirit is
  called away.
And we drape it in mourning wreaths.
To-day over thy Eastern home-nest, and over thy old home of the
  West.
A spirit of deepest sadness breathes :
The boat goes on, nor slacks its speed, yet many turn aside to
  heed
  The lov'd passenger that's missing,
And tears from many eyes are fulling, and that enchanting form
  recalling,
  Memory that dear face is kissing,

In the midst of antiquity and pleasures, surrounded by earthly
  treasures,
  Thou wert called to resign them all ;
But all know who knew thee, this side of the stormy sea,
  Thou wert ready for that sudden call.
In social groups there'll be a vacant seat, where thou used to
  meet,
  And round them hang a mournful spell.
Yet thou hast crossed life's stormy sea, but a trifle sooner than we
  Sister, whom we sadly whisper farewell.

CHICAGO, Sept. 15, 1874.

AND IS IT SO?

The following incidental poem is inscribed to the young lady who is the heroine of it, with the sympathy of the author who trusts that gentle hope may sometime be rewarded.

I READ it aloud—the love ditty—with its frank avowal of affection,
    Too sentimental, perhaps, for elderly people.
Yet being a waif from prized Bryant's collection,
    Though it climbed romance's bright steeple,
Petty aversion for once might undergo a removal,
And I looked accordingly, to read her approval.

But the eloquent, impassioned words that fell from my lips,
    Stirred not the face so patient and calmly serene;
And just as the frost the opening bud nips,
    Her blank look froze a fair cherished dream;
And its absence left a void Fate's gems may not fill;
A wild tumult, fair winds cannot still.

Her face was sweet with no vestige emotional,
    " And you don't believe in Love's castle erection ?"
She answered, " 'tis unreal, fanciful, notional,
    Man has no unselfish, undying affection;
There is but one love unimpassioned and mild,
'Tis a mother's perpetual love for her child.

" So-called love is a whimsical fancy or tumultuous passion,
  And dies like morning dew on the grass :"
And experienced echoed *such love is the fashion!*
  Encase the whole with oblivion's glass !
Yet as poem and dream I buried low,
Hope just *dared* whisper, and is it so ?

LET ME DIE IN MY YOUTH.

OH, let me die in my youth, ere the storm-clouds of life,
Mingled with the hurricanes of trouble and strife,
And the rough waves of this tempestuous cold world,
Have round my faltering footsteps been hurled,
Ere the sunlight fade wholly from out life's sky,
Let me die in my youth, in my youth let me die !

Ere those who love me have all passed away,   ·
And no fond, loving look near to me shall stay.
Ere smiles now so bright shall be dimmed by time,
Ere other voices sound sweeter than mine.
Ere love and affection fade from life's sky,
Let me die in my youth, in my youth let me die !

Ere I shall bury my hopes far out of sight,
Away from all future gleams of joy or light.
Ere brightest castles shall fall to sand,
Dark in the night of the past to stand,
Ere fond dreams fade from out of life's sky,
Let me die in my youth, in my youth let me die !

Ere low gentle words shall grow stern and cold,
Towards one that is faded, wrinkled and old,
Ere eyes meet mine no longer with joy,
But turn aside as from a broken toy,
Ere kind looks and words shall dim in life's sky,
Let me die in my youth, in my youth let me die!
CHICAGO, Sept. 12th, 1874.

ONE THING TO TALK AND ANOTHER TO DO.

OH, 'tis easy to talk, and for words to float out,
    As birds flit along on swift flying wings,
Brave, heroic deeds we can talk all about,
    But to talk, and to do, are two different things.

Promises are made, and in firm words spoken,
    But question how long will they last?
While one promise is made, two may be broken,
    For they are not with meditation o'ercast.

Promises were well, but they're easily made,
    Bright hopes for awhile they may strew,
But when fair castles fail, and bright seasons fade,
    We see 'twere easier to talk, than to do.

Then cheer not the heart with a promise that's brittle,
    For the sake of a sound that is fine,
Better than much, is the sure promised little,
    That comes in the opportune time.

Twere better to not build the bright castle at all,
  Than build on a promise that must soon slip thro,'
Than to see the phantom structure suddenly fall,
  For, 'tis *one thing* to talk, and *another* to do.

LOVE THAT WILL STEM FIRE AND WATER.

HER eyes are dark, and her face is fair,
And a garden of flowers resteth there,
Full lips of coral and hair of jet,
The rarest beauty eye hath seen yet,
Features and fortune all one could ask,
To like, admire, were an easy task
And love, we may add till from adversity's lake,
Eruptions of trials and failures break,
And then love seeks a more favorable quarter,
'Tis not the kind to stem fire and water.

Love sits not down o'er the eyes or hair,
Nor on the face tho' it be comely and fair.
Love perches not on the coral lips,
Nor into the bosom of fortune dips;
The hand may be large, or it may be small,
Does it matter to *love?* oh, not at all:
The mind may be strong, or weak as a dove,
Love is *love* because it is *love;*
Adversity'll not turn it in another quarter—
'Tis ready to stem both fire and water.

IN MEMORY OF DR. A. BEARDSLEY.

The Ocean of Life still glideth on the same,
   Yet on its shore of sand,
We miss a fair and faithful name,
   Shining on Heaven's strand.

One who hath walked with us many years,
   His good example e'er a guide,
Has left this world of care and tears,
   And crossed to the brighter side.

There's a vacant place where his footstep tread,
   The gentle voice we do not hear,
For he hath joined the happy dead,
   Where there's no sigh or tear.

Already he hath found the rest,
   For which *we* search o'er and o'er,
That genuine place that bears a test,
   Found only on that quiet shore.

While bitter tears are shed for him;
   Safe within jasper walls,
He's passed from a world of toil and sin,
   Away from temptation's calls.

And lo, a joy for each mourning friend,
　That beyond the rolling river,
Where life with its ups and downs shall end,
　Friends meet again together.

*　　*　　*　　*　　*　　*　　*

By ever that celestial city viewing,
　Shunning aught that may allure.
By ever the narrow way pursuing,
　Make Heaven's passport sure.

There's a pearly gate and a golden seat,
　Just beyond on that peaceful shore,
Where parted friends again may meet,
　And meet to part no more.

CLINTON, N. Y.

DUTY.

Written at the time of the Cuba altercation, and cry of war! and inscribed to a friend.

THERE'S many a bushy path that Duty bids us tread,
  And from them we would not turn aside,
Though their burdens be like weights of lead,
  If we be by conscience fully justified.
Through many channels we are called to pass,
  And through *some*, Duty may *seem* to call,
That when singled clearly from the mass,
  We find she toucheth not at all.

And there is the point, perhaps, on which we fail,
  Make ofttimes a fatal and sad mistake,
By *imagining* that Duty's sonorous calls assail,
  And thus morbid fancies oft awake,
When Duty points in an opposite direction,
  And we should strive to see her finger,
And not *fancy* that her mandate or connection,
  Near our names doth linger.

When o'er the water speeds the news afar,
  Raising fear, excitement and commotion,
The fearful, to-be-dreaded cry of war!
  When hearts are filled with quick emotion,

Let those pause awhile and think,
  On whom solemn, imposing duties rest,
Lest they should take a step on Danger's brink,
  That would be by God unblest

And those he hath designed for other, broader fields,
  Should not sever God's woven bands,
And take the swords and grasp the shields,
  Designed for use by other hands;
For there are those who cannot bring
  Salvation to fallen world and nation,
While they would better make the ring,
  To take the warrior's station.

Rush not headlong on for pastime or for pleasure,
  Be cautious, rather than audacious, bold,
For who the watery waves would measure,
  For paltry fame or shining gold?
Or who but to gain a valiant name,
  Cross the stormy waves to Cuba bound?
Or merely for popularity or brilliant fame,
  Find a grave on Spanish ground?

Thus admonishing would we speak to all,
  Especially the young and brave,
But wait, wait for the country's unmistaken call,
  Valor and effort for it save;
And *then*, if Duty at last demands,
  God's message "go," floats on the air,
With beating heart and trembling hands,
  We'll resign lov'd ones with a prayer.

WHO'D STRIVE?

WHO'D strive the joys of the present hour to hold,
Which must not only perish in the grasp
Of the next, but be succeeded by the fiercest opponents?

THITHER.

THITHER from uncertainty's turbulent waves to rest,
Like a frightened dove to its mother's breast.

WILL YOU THINK OF ME?

TO B. ——

AMONG the many and varied forms,
    Of all that you may see,
Mid life's thick and gathering storms,
    Where e'er you chance to be,
Mid life's fair or clouded morns,
    ll you ever think of me?

FORGIVE.

FORGIVE! nor number the times two, nor yet eleven,
Forgive! forgive even seventy times seven;
   Too much! Oh, too much, do I hear you say,
     As in prayer you bow the reverent head?
   Then every harsh thought, Oh, cast away,
     "Seventy times seven" the Saviour said.
   And mildly he looketh down from Heaven,
     And sayeth forgive, nor malice nor envy keep,
   Forgive as you hope to be forgiven,
     And how sweet will be your sleep!
We owe a debt which increases as long as we live,
As we would be forgiven, so let us forgive.

HER FATHER'S CHOICE.

A BALLAD OF FACT.

IN heart and spirit they were one, and loved each other well,
But the fickle hand of Fortune heavily upon them fell.

His forehead spoke of intellect, broad, and not too high,
And expressive, but mild and loving, was the keen blue eye

Too fair the brow the wealth of fair hair had shaded,
But for the firmness that every lineament pervaded.

In wealth of mind he stood far in advance of her relation,
Still unfortunate, for he chanced to be of humble station.

His clothes were not of broadcloth soft and fine,
He swung the scythe, and fed her father's kine.

Oft, when unobserved, she walked the meadow at his side,
And *bona fide* promised, to one day be his bride.

Happy they might have been, left to their own free choice,
But there broke in her father's unrelenting voice.

His irrevocable decision was, their union could not be,
He chose for her a bridegroom of noble birth and high degree

His choice, a wealthy neighbor's only son,
Two in God's sight, in wayward man's made *one.*

Betty stowed away her love in a silent little nook,
Nor dreamed they of the woful step she took.

Conscience said, "those vows are false, you'll rue the step you
        take;"
She responded, "not when I do it for my father's sake.

If she silently sighed for the true love she had won,
They only echoed, "how well she has done."

Years have passed on Time's ever progressive wave,
That father long has slept within his grave.

Gone her fortune that he with pride and boasting left.
Of her husband's care and love long since bereft.

Four children had blessed their once princelv home,
When he left her penniless and alone.

He left his home, his native land in shame,
A blackened stigma on his lofty name.

She, once beauty and belle, with many a wooer,
Now barely keeps starvation from the door.

She, once the gayest in the crowded festal room,
Earns a meager support at the weaver's loom.

And him whom oft she recalls in a dream,
Her youthful choice, perchance you have seen.

A minister who won a high station in which to preach,
His eloquence, thousands of hearts did reach.

Old and young would gather from far and near,
The youthful orator's impressive words to hear.

But his life was wrecked, and made drear and cold;
By one who sundered two hearts for gold.

An apology for love—he called two by name of wife,
And then in a fit of insanity, took his own life.

There comes a whisper, as 'twere a spirit voice,
" Ruin and suicide, the result of her father's choice."

TO MRS. DANIELS,

ON THE DEATH OF HER INFANT CHILD.

ONE summery day, a rosebud fair was blown,
But ere its perfume left a deepened trace,
It withered, and a signet cold was thrown
O'er its seraphic and heaven-lit face;
The bud of promise, so beauteous and fair,
Drooped, and ere long, dropped away;
But from thorny paths hedged in with Care,
It stepped into a long, perennial day;
From the shield of a warm, maternal breast,
Free from the harsh world's rust and canker,
It hath entered a haven of eternal rest,
Within the fold of a protecting anchor.

A picture with infantile beauty painted—
To what can it be in its purity allied?
Free from thought, by anxiety untainted,
By e'en a single frown unsullied,

Opened its little eyes, and closed in affection's clasp,
  On this variable and changeful scene,
Ere it strove the world's baubles to grasp,
  And find them all a dream.
Gone, beauteous messenger of the skies,
  Thy little life but a transient bubble;
Yet thou hast closed thy sinless eyes,
  On a landscape o'erhung with trouble.

We look sometimes, on one whose life is run,
  Perhaps, of three-score years and ten,
His life may have been a useful one,
  In the domestic circle, among his fellow men,
And the intricate labyrinths he has passed through,
  Were an example fair to leave;
But fairer the bud, unwet by chilling dew,
  That the Saviour without a question doth at once receive!
No strivings the heavenly crown to gain,
  Ah, no! the precious jewel has it free,
Instead of being tested in the gulf of grief and pain,
  Jesus said, " Let the little ones come unto me."

After a life of trial, struggle and exertion past,
  E'en with motives and endeavors all the best,
One almost doubts a right at last,
  To sink upon the loving Saviour's breast;
But the tiny and unspotted form
  Of one so gloriously radiant and fair,
Its life but a fair unclouded morn,
  Must the richest blessings share;

While the fond earthly tie is torn asunder,
   There is a happy thought connected,
Fair bud united to a joyous number,
   That e'er will be well protected.

SWEET HOUR OF PRAYER.

ANOTHER day with its petty toils is o'er,
And joined to those that have gone before,
And tho' far from the valley I love so well,
Far from my own loved favorite dell,
I know as I drink the evening air,
'Tis the hour of seven—the hour of prayer.

And o'er the distant miles that lie between,
O'er the broad expanses that intervene,
In that chapel warm and bright,
My heart is with you friends, to-night.
Ah, yes, though far away, I meet you there,
To spend with you this hour of prayer.

Now rises the prayer of humble confession,
A hymn follows next in succession,
Then words of love and sweet truth are spoken,
A band connected too close to be broken,
Ah, in that Chapel so cheerful, so fair,
At this hour of seven, I meet you there.

TO BUNKER-HILL MONUMENT.

OH, ye silent monitor of granite, towering high.
At whose basis a thousand memories lie ;
  How names dim but for history's pages,
Come thronging in one vast line,
  Names that glowed in by-gone ages,
O'ershadowed by the wings of time ;
Ah, the names of those who responded to their country's call,
And bravely on the battle-field did fall.

To the dust, long since mingled with its kindred clay,
Memory bears a tribute here to-day ;
  Ah, step lightly on this sacred soil,
And deem it a privilege and a treat,
  For tired with heat, o'ercome with toil,
Here walked brave Warren's feet ;
We climb thy cold stone steps and think of those
Whose hearts and spirits with heroic valor rose.

Six hundred and twenty-two feet from earth we stand,
In this marble monument tall and grand ;
  And gratitude surges quick and fast,
Through every pulsing vein,
  Far up through the vestibule of the past,
We see the Revolutionary stain,
Through dim time, descendants see it still,
And who will e'er forget the battle of Bunker Hill.

CHARLESTOWN, MASS.

THE TWO BEARS.

THERE are two bears that near us we should allow to dwell,
Nor e'er by harsh word or hasty act repel,
Homes and lives can only be happy made,
   Where these two bears are allowed to stay,
And the foundation for enjoyment is laid,
   Where these two bears haunt the way.
Oh, send them never crossly from the door,
But let them remain one's sight before,
For they'll ne'er bring grief nor sorrow,
   Nor ever a thought of pending sadness,
They'll point out many a bright to-morrow,
   And fill it with joy and gladness,
Those two bears we should nourish e'er with care,
Their names, remember, are Bear and Forbear.

A YEAR.

TIME goes sailing on, nor slacketh speed,
Nor weeks, nor months doth stop to heed,
Sweeping o'er seasons like a passing dream,
Changing many a fair and beauteous scene,
Cheered by its smile, watered by its tear,
There standeth by, the twelfth season near,
            Another year!

The brooklet its merry song still singing,
The bird his diurnal visit bringing,
Trees loaded with blossoms in the spring,
Precious fruit in fall they bring.
The leaves are green, then brown and sere,
Showing that autumn draweth near,
           Gone a year!

We turn one glance adown the flowery dell,
To bid, we think, a brief farewell,
Press the lips from which we must part,
Whisper with lov'd ones pressed to our heart,
List'ing to the voice like music to our ear,
Scanning the faces that are to us so dear,
          "Only a year!"

Oh, fickle, fateful, e'er changeful Time,
That variest all within thy line,
Wilt make changes 'mid the scenes we leave,
And o'er them a mournful chasm weave?
Wilt leave the eyes now bright and clear,
And the forms to us so loved and dear,
          'Til we return in a year?

SUNSHINE AND SHADOW.

OFT morning's brightest sunshine pales,
　　Long hours before the night,
And many a dense and misty shadow veils
　　The brilliant rays of early light;
Yet while the dazzling sunbeams met the eye,
　　We quaffed the joy they brought,
And when we see how soon they die,
　　We read the lesson taught.

A lesson for Life is typified by Day,
　　And we start with prospects bright,
Soon, perhaps, to see them swept away,
　　And vanished from our sight:
Thus oft we're hailed by dark Despair,
　　Motioned towards her waters deep,
Because our temples bright and fair,
　　Lie shattered at our feet.

Bringing *fact*, instead of *fancy*, to our view,
　　We see many a castle rent asunder,
Crushed, and broken through and through,
　　And bright names were of that number;

Of Love, and Joy, and Hope and Trust,
  But lo, we wake with a sudden start,
To find prostrate and crumbled in the dust,
  The fair idols of our heart.

How often the casket of our hopes is broken,
  And its precious contents spilled,
Leaving scarce one testimonial token,
  Of the jewels with which 'twas filled;
And if Fate grows harsher still and sterner,
  And our dearest treasures perish,
We know, though we sigh and murmur,
  Earthly idols we should not cherish.

We may prize our gems from Fortune's hand,
  Love our friends God-given,
But dwelling, too, on a safer strand,
  With our brightest tho'ts of Heaven.
Many and tempestuous are the storms of life,
  While its thorns are not a few,
But looking aloft o'er the field of strife,
  There's One will lead us through.

Shadows all through our life will come,
  We couldn't dispel them if we would,
And perhaps 'twere better not to be done,
  For their presenee may do us good:
For were our lives, lives of sunshine quite,
  Without a shadow here and there,
Soon, we shouldn't appreciate the brightest light,
  But deem it, as a matter of course, our share.

Life is a blending of sunshine and showers,
  One from the other we cannot well single,
December's snow and May's gorgeous flowers,
  In forming the seasons must mingle;
Thus when dark clouds obscure the way,
  For death we would not yearn,
But hopeful wait for a fairer day,
  Take sunshine and shadow in turn.

LINES ON RECEIVING A BOUQUET OF HOUSE-PLANTS.

TO MRS.——

My friend, many long miles between us stand,
  But Fancy, thy kind face can see,
Lo! the lovely bouquet that's placed in my hand,
  And she pictures her who formed it for me ;
And o'er the miles Imagination all swiftly flies,
  To greet you, my friend, with a kiss,
Trifling act, you say; yet never dies
  The sweet memory connected with this.
Each little blossom how dearly I prize,
  As I gaze at it o'er and o'er.
For each brings before my enraptured eyes,
  Her who held it before.
I shall preserve it, Oh, how careful and choice
  And though faded and withered it be,
Oft I'll picture the face and the silvery voice,
  Of her who sent it to me.

ANNA, THE WASHERWOMAN'S DAUGHTER.

NOON-TIME in Madame L's fashionable boarding school,
  And a bevy of girls most light of heart, and gay,
Pour forth into the June air, soft and cool,
  And in varied directions take their way.

In friendly groups and knots they gather,
  With " Oh, you're going my way to-day !
Good ! I hope to-morrow'll be jolly weather!
  Going, aren't you, Sue and May ?"

And they launch on the current theme—the party,
  With an exhibition of amicable caresses,
And picture with zeal and enthusiasm hearty,
  Their respective ties and dresses.

And chatty words fall from the lips of those
  Who, except theoretically, know naught of sorrow,
And none of life's harsh wants or cruel woes,
  Have ever dimmed their bright to-morrow.

But look! behold that girl so slight and frail !
  For, ah, she knows both want and care,
Though her slender form and face so pale,
  Show her too young and fair.

And lo, she lingers as all the school retreats!
  Sadly she stays alone, and wherefore?
Plainly, 'tis but to brush the dusty seats,
  And sweep the school-room floor.

And doing this, aspiring Anna cancels her tuition,
  She rings the bell, and passes water,
And discards the words—with her ambition—
  " Anna, the Washerwoman's daughter."

Unceasing time sweeps on, nor rests, nor pauses,
  And Madame L's hundred girls or more
Have stepped into life's sentences and clauses.
  And Anna, who swept the school-room floor.

But they grasp the literary records, be life sad or gay,
  And search in their homes in every quarter,
For words of the inspiring author of the day,
  " Anna, the Washerwoman's daughter."

THE BRIGHT SIDE.

THERE's many a sunbeam behind a cloud,
  And smooth waves after rough tide,
When the weather is bleak and the winds are loud,
  We'll look on the brightest side.

The ups and downs of this life are many,
  But the joys obscured from sight,
By trials and troubles unknown to any,
  Are continually brought to light.

CLOSE OF THE YEAR 'SEVENTY-THREE.

WRITTEN FOR A READING.

ANOTHER year on wingéd wings has fled away,
  Its hours are almost o'er,
When we behold a new-born day,
  'Twill be in the year of 'seventy-four.
The year hath its joys and sorrows brought,
  The latter, we'd with the year let die,
The former be with memory fraught,
  E'er in her golden frame to lie.

The year hath bro't its seasons of cold and heat,
    Seed-time sowing and harvest reaping,
Fortune some with smiling face doth greet,
    But poverty o'er the land is sweeping.
There hath been the marriage bells' gay jingle,
    And the wail of the infant child,
Alike the funeral knell's sad mingle,
    'Mid the chaos of confusion wild.

While here to-night, a warm, united band,
    My friends, let's covenant and agree,
To remember suffering ones thoughout our land,
    The stricken ones of 'seventy-three;
And bear to the throne of grace to-night,
    Tho' remembrance be to them unspoken,
Those family circles that once were bright.
    But now, alas, are broken.

Many who entered with us on this same year,
    Have with the dead been numbered,
Many beloved by us and to us dear,
    In death long since have slumbered;
Now as we verge on the year that's at the door,
    One word I would speak to all,
Just as we part, perchance to meet no more—
    Let's strive to meet in yon jasper Hall.

My friends, I trust that the year that now is dawning,
    May bring you blessings good and true,
That within its clasp many a sunny morning,
    Be waiting there for you;

Yet while joy's cup you almost grasp,
  Know sorrow may lurk below,
And though you drink, and e'en it clasp,
  Be ready, too, to let it go.

We turn one tho't down the vista of the past,
  Another, on the Future's shore unknown,
And may God with his mercy e'er o'ercast,
  Wherever we are thrown;
And guard us wherever we may be,
  · His oil of light upon us pour,
This we ask as we bid farewell to 'seventy-three,
  And welcome the year of 'seventy-four.

ON THE DEATH OF FANNIE CURRIE.

WHILE the noisy world goes on for aye,
  · Nor slacketh its commotion,
We turn our thoughts aside to-day,
  Filled with deep emotion;
For Death our little glen hath entered,
  And another lain to slumber,
O'er one his mantle swiftly centered,
  Bright jewel of our number.

Though tears fall fast from many an eye,   ·
  For her whom God had loaned,   ·
In mansions fair beyond the sky,
  The loved one sits enthroned.
There's a vacant place in that household left,
  That we know will long remain,
But, mourning friends, who've been bereft,
  Your loss is the angels' gain.

Through murmuring breezes of the air
  There sadly comes a sigh,
For, to one beloved and fair,
  We are called to bid good-bye;
When with mingled joys and sorrows past,
  Our struggling lives have flown,
May we in heaven meet thee at last,
  Where parting is unknown.

CLINTON, N. Y.

SUPERSTITION.

"MAMMA was with me," said I, "in my dream,
  "And clasped me in her loving arms,
And no misty shadows were there between,
  To dim the sweetest of maternal charms."

" Oh," says a dream teller, full of false superstition,
  " To dream of the living is sign of a death,"
And down went the castles of my fairest ambition,
  As goes a bubble blown by a breath

My dream that surely did with happiness inspire
  Met with such a perilous fall,
So appalling, so dreadful, so dire,
  'Twere better I had not dreamed it at all.

When thro' the clouds stole a bright ray,
  False doctrines ye hearers believe not,
All superstition put ye away,
  There's One who appointeth our lot.

And when later I felt my mother's warm clasp,
  I raised my eyes to my Father above,
If e'er superstition would hold me in grasp,
  May I look to Thy mercy, Thy love.

SNOW FLAKES.

Soft and white they fall one by one,
Melting at first in the rays of the sun,
Thus the foundation for drifts is begun,
  By small, white snow-flakes.

Mildly they float through the cold, frosty air,
Pure, unpolluted, lovely and fair,
Falling, the dirt of the street to share,
    The pure, white snow-flakes.

Down to kiss the faces they meet,
Down to sit at the harsh world's feet,
To cover the earth with their snowy sheet,
    The pure, innocent snow-flakes.

But lo! when they reach the broad highway,
No longer pure and white they stay;
But mingle with filth and mud and clay,
    A pile of soiled snow-flakes.

And surely it needs watchfulness and care,
To keep our lives as pure and fair,
As the snow-flakes flying through the air,
    The pure, white snow-flakes.

LINES TO WILLARD.

WILLARD, dearest cousin of my heart,
    The prolonged hours of my stay
    Have glided, glided swift away,
The hour draws nigh for us to part.

Cousin of my affection fond and true,
  Deep emotions fill my breast,
  Brightest tokens of love's test,
As I pen these parting lines for you.

With joy we meet, with sadness part,
  And hoping joy for you in store,
  That happiness lay your life before,
I try to soothe my aching heart

That an untruth ne'er on thy lip may lie,
  That your life may be e'er pure and fair,
  Is my heartfelt, earnest prayer,
As I bid you, cousin dear, good-bye.

STAR OF HOPE.

WE look o'er the dark clouds that hover around,
  To greet a ray of light visible afar,
And tho' trials and troubles are dense and profound,
  We would look for Hope's radiant star.

Dark days we know must come unto all,
  But we ne'er should give up to despair,
While we can look o'er the fierce waterfall,
  To a star that's so bright and so fair.

The tempest of life is a fierce, howling blast,
　Yet sweet, hidden joys it may bar,
The sweeping tide fair gems may o'ercast,
　Bro't to light by Hope's radiant star.

Let's not frown on what misfortunes have severed,
　Not their fair inherent beauties mar,
By omitting the value there is to be gathered,
　By looking at Hope's wondrous star.

THE WAY IN WHICH HE LEADS US.

OFT thro' by-paths and strange we find our footsteps pacing,
　Where we see little of joy to feed us,
But though shades of darkness we may be facing,
　'Tis the way in which He leads us.

And tho' the paths are those we should not choose,
　We know He'll guide and feed us ;
Then should we follow on, nor e'er refuse
　The way in which He leads us.

AUNTIE, GOOD-BYE.

THE last month of the year, just before we drop a tear
      O'er his frosty, algid bier,
      And with it a sigh,
Thou hast entered the mystic portals, bless'd abode of the
      Auntie, good-bye.   [immortals;

We shall know thee here no more, nor when weary miles we've
      See thy face at the door,   [speeded o'er,.
      When we draw nigh;
Thy feet no more will run, to 'note joy that we have come;
      Auntie, good-bye.

Thy hand will no more caress, nor forehead fondly press,
      As if silently to bless
      Life's protean sky;
How easy rent the vital spark which leaves this world so dark!
      Auntie, good-bye.

Still in thy blest abode, bless if thou may the hoary load,
      Met in Life's weary road;
      Thy pet would cry
'Twere no task to weep at will, would it keep the wrung heart
      Auntie, good-bye.   [still;.

Across the slight division, into a perennial elysium,
    To thee a sweet transition;
    If thou mayst, from on High,
Smile on the friends thou'st left bowed deeply and bereft;
    Auntie, good-bye.

CHICAGO, December 18, 1874.

ANGEL OF COMFORT.

STORMS may rage and the winds may blow,
Sorrows may come and joys may go,
The heart be crushed 'neath burdens of care,
Even Hope be defied by despair,
'Mid adversity's dull drenching showers,
May be seen no bright up-springing flowers,
Still there's *one* can banish resentment,
And scatter roses of sweetest contentment,
Ope' the heart's door nor drive him away,
For he'll brighten even the darkest day,
    'Tis Patience, the Angel of Comfort.

Ah, sorrowing one with the downcast eye,
Not wishing to live, but asking to die,
Naught but misfortunes around you have coiled,
Your bravest efforts have only been foiled,
Your noblest aims have met with repulsion,
Fate yields not to prayer or compulsion,

The wide world passes you coldly,
You ask its assistance, it stares at you boldly,
With all your pure aims and motives so true,
It jostles you rudely, there's nothing for you.
  Behold Patience, the Angel of Comfort!

You've made promises impossible to meet,
Friends no longer see you when in the street,
Adversity, Friendship's most pointed test,
Has affected those who loved you the best.
"Prosperity's the very heart of love,"
Which afflictions soon can remove;
But tho' a channel where mystery lurks,
God, his mighty wonder sure works,
Welcome, then, that one consoling friend,
"Most poor matters point to some rich end."
  Welcome Patience, the Angel of Comfort!
CHICAGO, Jan. 16th, 1875.

REQUIESCAT IN PACE.

Gen. A. C. Harding died in Monmouth, Warren Co., Ill., July
19, 1874.

ROUND us on every side we still behold the rolling world,
 Its bustling business and confusion on every side,
But we pause amid vicissitudes at our feet now hurled,
 To give a tribute tho't to him crossed o'er the mystic tide.

The world still has its men both good and great,
  Yet the *world* should drop a tear o'er this one of its number,
But oh, remembrance and gratitude of *this western* state,
  Should ne'er in the future be known to slumber.

Prominent among the names on this century's page,
  Thr'out the world, first thr'out the western land,
The name honored and revered of this belov'd and model sage,
  Ah, bright and beautiful will the name of Gen. Harding stand!

Remember him, ye agéd, forget him not, ye young,
  Tho' aside from earth's routine of months he be lain,
Bless him for that sonorous voice that oft has rung,
  Bless him for the iron cars that scour the plain.
And let his precepts e'er on fancy's wing be strung,
  And while the result of his good words we see,
We say to this world's prized friend, *Requiescat in pace!*

LOVE VERSUS RICHES.

In a stately mansion that wealth had decked with care,
Sat the lovely heiress—the spoiled coquette—Irene LaClare
In her mind she was revolving o'er and o'er,
The suitors that thronged her by the tens and score;

And among all who to her charms had bowed,
She loved but *one*, yet she was proud,
And he was poor, but of noble mind, and good,
Still framed in her mind her *ideal lover* stood—
Wealthy, intellectual, of noble birth and grand,
And only *he* could aspire to that fair hand !

And while thus she mused, through the carvéd door,
Came her lover *rich*, yet to worldly eyes so poor,
And after a lingering silence that reigned around,
'Mid an embarrassment deep, profound,
To the tho'ts that lay uppermost in his mind,
His lips an utterence were forced to find :
Down; down she crushed the rising love—
His eloquence that proud heart must not move,
Should he *win*, with nothing but *merit* on which to stand,
While she'd been sought by the highest of the land?

He was her equal by talent and connection,
While he'd gained her purest and best affection,
But there was Pride standing ever near to warn her,
Of the lack of wealth and the deficient corner;
And from her, proud and sorrowful he turned away,
And left the town that had been so bright, so gay ;
And ere a year had passed with its gentle glide,
He had won a young and lovely bride,
And ere another flitting year had fled,
Irene La Clare slept with the dead.

THE BELLE OF LONG BRANCH.

AGAIN I seek the rustic seat upon the tented beach,
  Where I sat two years ago—ah, well!
Ah, Memory why now o'er past realms reach,
  To recall the Long Branch Belle?
Yes, on this spot, the white robed flitted by,
  And then the hard gained introduction,—
A seaside flirt, a heartless coquette you cry,
  Who wrought my life's destruction!

There you're wrong, revoke the harsh decision,
  She was true to me as steel,
And would have made my life elysian
  But now I must sorrow and anguish feel;
For there is a brighter world than this,
  A world that is more genial, fair,
A haven of rest of long, perennial bliss,
  And she was wanted there.

And now I watch the faces of dazzling beauty,
  In haunts aside from the scorching sun,
And conscience whispers—it is your duty—
  There's none like that lost one:
Hers was a heart too pure, a nature too lovely far,
  For this earth's cold, dismal spell,
I fancy her awaiting me—my Life's Star,
  The beauteous Long Branch Belle.

FALLEN CASTLES.

CASTLES how oft they're built by the young, the brave, the fair,—
Built with a strong, ambitious hand,
O'erhung with caution, and inlaid with care,
How firm they may seem to stand!
But though they're built with many a spacious hall,
The most elaborate built may be the first to fall.

In this battle-field of life, with its varied ups and downs,
We see the wrecks on every hand,
Where bright castles stood awhile amid life's frowns,
Then fell, worthless, to the sand:
Phantom structures that briefly cheered life's pathway,
Then vanished into dim and dark decay.

How many, looking into the chambers of the past,
See, lying amid the chaos there,
Though with the lines of care and time o'ercast,
A fallen castle that once was fair:
A castle that once was bright, and gilded gay,
That by some slight jostling was swept away.

CHICAGO, Sept. 29, 1874.

THE CARRIER'S CALL.

ONE of the brightest episodes of city life,
  Of its eventful incidents, great or small,
For which we wait and listen amid the strife,
  Is surely the Carrier's call.

Hark ! there's the Carrier on his morning round,
  Yet stay ! he calls but *one name* this time—
Eager ears listen with interest profound,
  And to each, it sounds like *mine.*

The Carrier bringeth glad tidings and fun,
  And some sweet message to all :—
What sound is as universal a welcome one,
  As the Carrier's sonorous call ?

Welcome, yes, welcome up avenue and street,
  And while we rush for mail in a *whew,*
Let's not forget with a smile to greet
  The Public's ambassador faithful and true !

As cheery an episode, we venture to say,
  As may be in the storehouse of Memory's hall,
In the coming hours of a future day,
  Will be the Carrier's call.

CHICAGO, Oct. 10, 1874.

PAPA'S HAIR.

" Little Jessie's growing handsome, Mrs. Blue,
    Complexicn like yours, so clear and fair,
Then she laughs so much like you,
    But she's got her father's hair."

Jessie sat in the window with flowers tied,
    To form a garland and floral gem—
" Well ! if I've got papa's hair," she cried,
    " It's why *he* wears a wig, then !',

A HIT ON YOUNG AMERICAS.

"I'D like to go to China and Japan, mother,
    Teach that benighted race the light to see,
How I'd joy to watch their progress,
    What a glorious mission it would be !
To hear them read and see them write,
    Oh, 'twould be fun for me."

" But Mary, there are children here,
    Children plenty within your reach,
There's mission work this side the Ocean,
    Just you do instead of preach. "
" Yes, mother, there *are* children *here*,
    But *they're* to wild for me to teach."

THANKSGIVING DAY.

THE seasons have formed another year which now has cycled
    round,
    Again November's blasts sweep fiercely o'er the way,
And amid the merry sleigh bells' sound,
    We welcome another Thanksgiving Day,—
We drink its joys, nor count its sorrows o'er,
And memorize Thanksgiving Day of Eighteen seventy-four.

This day to *some*, in Memory's hall will brighter stand,
    Will intimation do or must we say,
That for those who resign their heart and hand,
    On this Thanksgiving Day,
For those, Memory in her hallowed store,
Will record Thanksgiving Day, Eighteen seventy-four.

Young and old, come forth and proudly stand,
  To shout a welcome and joyful lay,
Yet dark clouds have o'erswept our land,
  Since last Thanksgiving Day—
Clouds of death, and fire, and scandal have touched life's sea,
Since Thanksgiving Day Eighteen seventy-three.

Aside from the thousands of lives on life's vast battle-field,
  Reviewing personal changes that have dimmed life's sky to grey,
Fortune hath not been slow his fickle wand to wield,
  Since last Thanksgiving Day !
Still may our land with many a blessing thrive,
For all who see Thanksgiving Day of Eighteen seventy-five !
  CHICAGO, Nov. 26, 1874.

TWO RINGS OF A LIFETIME.

" BUT, Grandma, didn't you wear rings when you were young ?"
  Raising her tiny hand—five rings in a line—
A hand that was shapely and too small by far,
  To be decked with jewels so costly and fine.

"Wear rings, my child ? yes, but the only ones ever I wore—
  Though perhaps 'twas only a fancy of mine,
I know that you'll think I should have worn more—
  But I never wore but two rings in my life-time.

"They're in that little box in the drawer—no, child, it's blue,—
　Yes, here they are, you see they are not fine,
But still, if you wish, I'll give their history to you,
　Only think of two rings in a long life-time

"My father was rich—I might have had rings a score,
　But over that subject how fancy would linger,
And child, the first ring that ever I wore,
　Your Grandfather Thomas put on my finger.

"And—ah, yes, he was poor, and the ring was a plain one,
　And father—I'm only too sorry to tell—
Would have had me secure him a wealthier son,
　And a ring more brilliant as well.

"My father's irate countenance I fancy I'm seeing,
　And yet 'tis fondly memory doth linger,
For amid all his frowns I was the happiest being,
　The day this ring was placed on my finger.

"Father got quiet—called it a girlish fancy, a bubble,
　I was a trifle over nineteen, you see,
Then it was thought to foreshadow a life of trouble,
　To promise your hand ere seeing twenty.

"Not much like that Saratoga Miss falling in love at ten!
　Then households were free from riotous clatter,
But now children fall into love (?) and fall out again,
　And make no bones over the matter.

"And if they'd fall out before rushing into matrimony's arms,—
But then Divorce Courts would go down,
And without these hovering and perilous alarms,
There'd be dullness in city and town.

"For years our paths were wide apart—but he, I will not linger,
Six years! and *his* ring *alone* was mine,
And then one day he placed *another* on my finger,
And these are the two rings of a life time."

KNITTING SCARLET WORSTED.

KNITTING, knitting, knitting there in the cabin door,
On sped the weary fingers, for she was poor,
The scarlet zephyr flew in, and swiftly flew out,
As she weighed and counted, with many a doubt,
The flour and meat the work would buy,
And then over the worsted there fell a sigh,—
Nor little dreamed, as she fastened each scarlet thread,
She fastened a heart in the folds of the web.

And the knitting went wearily on from chime to chime,
Tired fingers found no sweet resting time,
Nor yet did the evening her cares at all diminish,
'Twas work, work, work, with never a finish;

But the last rays of the day's setting sun,
Fell over the tidy, charmingly done,—
Nor dreamed, as she laid it aside that August day,
In its meshes she folded a heart away.

And many was the gem of scarlet she netted beside,
That took the lead, and all others defied,
And so she worked still, from morning till night.
Did she wish for a path more dewy and bright?
No murmuring complaints her life e'er attended,
For precious lives on her efforts depended,—
Nor dreamed that the web she had woven and sold,
Still held a heart in its scarlet fold.

And years went on, and she was a lady fair,
Lightly touched by the lines of care,
While to science and art she was not blind,
For she had stored with care her fertile mind ;
And then, at last, there came a day,
She never had dreamed could be so gay,
When she joined her heart with all love's store,
To the one she had knit long years before.

WORKING AND WAITING.

OH, the thousands of feet that are dragging along,
   And the hands that are toiling away,
In cities and towns where hundreds of laborers throng,
   Working and waiting to-day.

Working and waiting, and thus years go by,
  And time his iron teeth keeps grating,
And many see hope's sun set in life's sky,
  But still keep working and waiting!

And when the last ray of light goes out, forever
  Sinks behind a brave, towering hill,
Be also those patient hands unfaltering never,
  But working and waiting still.

A WOMAN'S HAND!

NEITHER size, shape, nor color, come in demand,
To form the beauty of a woman's hand.
To prize but a faultless shape and snowy shade,
Were to admire beauty that soon may fade;
While the darkest hand and the homeliest one,
May have many a deed of kindness done;
The plainest one we say may have gained lines of beauty,
By unflinchingly performing deeds of duty;
That plain brown hand just you raise it up,
And say it shall dash aside the wine cup,
And lo, its beauty ineffable and untold,
Far surpasses brilliant gems of shining gold;
But let the fairest hand offer the wine cup to a human being,
And there's no beauty in it worth the seeing.

But you, with a hand that's comely and fair,
Know good or evil is clinging there;
And surely the responsibility is greater still,
Of that hand whose beckoning is law and will.
Oh, the power, thrilling, magnetic, effectual and grand,
Concealed in the effort of a woman's hand,
Providing that hand, be it carefully understood,
Be one that carries a sublime shield of good!
Nor think too good that fair and shapely hand,
To wipe human blood from ruin's sand,
To extend to that perilous and disgusting track,
And drag poor, demented beings back!
Guardian angels, as it were, may stand,
Enveloped in one pure and stainless hand;
But while those far down the hill we would fain secure,
One ounce of *prevention* will offset two of *cure;*
Then let's work at the bottom of the drunkard's gutter,
Full of sin and vice too wofully sad to utter,
While we may perhaps with just cause doubt,
If woman's hand could pull them out,
Her hand may turn aside the cup of sin,
And keep them, better still, from falling in.
There's a call for the virtuous women throughout our land,
Let every woman raise a hand!

MY HEART IS BREAKING.

SONG.

My heart is breaking, ah, yes, it is breaking,
　Breaking with its burden of sorrow!
I fall asleep and dread morning's waking,
　For sadder seems each to-morrow :
My heart is breaking, Oh, yes, it is breaking,.
　Nor is it delusion I borrow!

My heart is breaking, ah, yes, it is breaking,
　Why break poor heart so young?
When the dimness of age is o'ertaking,
　And the heart with care hath been wrung,
'Twere easier then to feel joy forsaking,
　When the Song of Life had been sung.

My heart is breaking, ah, yes, it is breaking,
　And why in the morning of life?
To be perhaps long on Life's voyage awaking,
　Amid its wild tumults and strife,
No ray of light to be music making,
　Where dark frowns must ever be rife!

My heart is breaking, ah, yes, it is breaking,
  'Neath a weight of premature care,
And sadness is swiftly o'ertaking,
  A life that was once so fair—
But hark, a message of gladness, there's no mistaking,
  Breaks on the still evening air.

AT NIGHT.

TIME, when the world with its weary cares and insidious sn;
With its smiles and frowns, and ups and downs,
With its harsh words cold, and stares so bold,
With its many a mansion, and lovers of fashion,
With its hovels and huts, and scornful cuts,
With its few generous hands, to reach where Worth stands,
With its tired brains, its losses and gains,
With its aching hearts, its cruel darts,
With its steam of prosperity, its wheels of adversity,
Time, when the weary world, by Fate's finger twirled,
Bars its factory door for the rich and the poor,
From the Squire to the Clerk, all rest from their work,
And the world is shut in by a door whose hinges are light,
And the name of this door is the beautiful Night.

THE CASTLE OF CARDS.

TRANSLATED AND TRANSFORMED FROM THE FRENCH.

In a quiet spot away from vexation and noise,
Lived a man, his good wife and two pretty boys;
In the spot, where, with peace around their door,
Their parents and ancestral friends had lived before.
Here with the sweet breath domestic can throw,
They watched their sons in knowledge grow:
The eldest was studious and full of thought,
The youngest, cared for sports, his books were naught;
One evening, all around the fireside seated,
The eldest read Rollin, that of ancient Romans treated,
Suddenly, with a burst from enthusiasm's well,
"The difference between founders and conquerors, please father
    tell."
The youngest, who cared not for history's bards,
Was vigorously building a castle of cards,—
Behold at this moment the frail castle stand,
When lo, it falls by a knock from his brother's hand.
The father, contemplating for an answer a sage one,
Replied, "your brother's the founder, you are the conquerer, my
    son."

SOMEWHERE, SOMETIME.

INTO this bustling world of storm,
That child, perhaps, is not yet born,
  Who shall see intemperance banished;
Yet we would ne'er the cause resign,
  But still strive to have it vanished,
It will be conquered *somewhere, sometime !*

We may wearily plant trees for falling brothers,
Nor see them eat the fruit—but may not others?
  Then let us sow seed, though others may reap,
Willing bands scatter good seeds in a line,
  For though we may have fallen asleep,
'Twill bear fruit *somewhere, sometime!*

Intemperence! its insidious danger strive to tell!
'Tis told by saying: Just imagine hell!
  Toward quelling this evil, sisters, friends,
Let every effort and power incline,
  For every firm step taken surely tends,
To quench it *somewhere, sometime !*

IN THE ARBOR AT THE FOOT OF THE GARDEN.

DAYS have made months, and months have rolled into 'years,
 And twenty or more have glided away,
Since I left my childhood's home, with its smiles and its tears,
 Left it for the city so dazzling and gay.
Now I am back again—I'll to some favorite nook—
 But ah, time the affections may not harden—
Then *first* I seek, not the barn, the well or the brook,
 But the arbor at the foot of the garden!

Why this spot of all others do I thus quickly single?
 Ah, 'tis a sad little story, but true,
And though gray hairs with black ones now mingle,
 I'll venture to lift the curtain for you:
Why do I seek this sequestered, moss-grown tent?
 Life's happiest hour—that time may not harden—
Memory unwavering assures me was spent,
 In the arbor at the foot of the garden!

I was a country girl, ignorant of aught but labor,
 But I had ambition which I was bound to cherish,
Tom Hoffman was my lover, playmate and neighbor,
 And ours was love that could not perish.
Twenty years have come and as many have fled,
 Since that scene, time may not harden,
I told him the project I had in my head,
 In the arbor at the foot of the garden.

I see his face now through a channel of twenty years,
  Ah, 'tis firmly stamped on memory's page,
And I see it through a misty sea of tears;
  I am called an " Eminent Woman of the Age,"
But I'd resign to-day all the fame I have gained,
  For time, the affection cannot wholly harden,
Though it be blotted, and blurred and stained—
  To see *him* in the arbor at the foot of the garden !

Time has swallowed years since that golden hour,
  And youth and ambition no longer are rife,
The girl who sat in the vine-wreathed bower,
  Is a woman now in the noon of life ;
Some events are past, to be recalled no more,
  But there's *one*, time may not harden,
'Tis that parting scene at the hour of four,
  In the arbor at the foot of the garden !

OVER THE HILLS IN BERRY TIME.

MEMORY flies back a score of years,
  And there are fences we used to climb,
As merrily, gayly, blithly, we pranced,
  Over the Hills in berry time !

Ah, what spruce old times we used to have,
  Jamie and Bell, and cousin Lime,
Some of life's bright hours were spent,
  Over the hills in berry time.

Then there came a day in riper years,
  When I gave my heart to cousin Lime,
But surely we first learned to love,
  Over the hills in berry time!

And Bell has wedded a gay Attorney,
  Adapted to the wreaths of romance she'd twine,
With a pail of fruit and a book of rhymes,
  Over the hills in berry time!

And Jamie, ah, there's a tear as I write,
  For those fairy feet that used to climb—
Ah, absent one of our number!
  Over the hills in berry time!

MILKING THE COWS.

No, you'd hardly think by my hands, friends,
  My hands so soft and white,
That I once drove cows from pasture,
  And milked a score at night.

Then when I went to bed, I slept,
  Nor woke till daylight's dawning,
And Fredie called the cows up,
  And I had but twelve for morning.

Then I was hungry, and how good it seemed,
  To hear the breakfast bell ring loud,
And I walked in with Fredie,
  Feeling womanly and proud.

Then life was sweet, ah, sweet indeed,
  You wonder now, it is not fair?
I was not born, too late, I know,
  For the wife of a millionaire.

Beside that milk-pail, stool and vis-à-vis,
  These estates are but a broken toy,
I'd give them all for Fredie,
  Who was once my father's chore boy!

THE HAND WITHOUT THE HEART.

Of all the "might have beens" so sad to read on memory's page,
  One seemeth sadder far than all the rest,
For it banishes faith and hope from out the heart,
  There, ne'er more to make their nest.

Listen, ye youth, throughout our proud progressive land!
  We beg your close and kind attention,
For it is expressly for your joy and welfare,
  We of this sad note make mention

The saddest " might have been " we so calmly read,
  That forms of life a part,
Is to pledge the hand, before the altar,
  Reserving still, the faithful heart.

I've lived a life of two score years and ten,
  And I, one cloudy, far off day,
Blighted my life by hugging my heart,
  And giving my hand away.

There are marriages for wealth and station,
  And I was poor and proud,
So I kept my heart and gave my hand,
  While conscience clamored loud.

But there came a time, I gave my heart,
  My hand was bound, but heart was free,
And thus the two were severed,
  Dear reader, pity me!

And so the years have slipped away,
  And the hand has been true and fulfilled its **part**,
But ah! the saddest " might have been,"
  Is the hand without the heart.

Now youthful fair, throughout our land,
    In that crisis step that must joy or grief impart,
Beware! nor e'er bestow the hand,
    Till likewise you give the heart.

DEAD ON A BED OF ROSES.

The Continental Herald says : The corpse of a young lady was recently found in the Valley of Rosegg, extended on a bed of Alpine roses, Oct. 11, 1874.

ONE of the mysteries that so oft occur,
    Where the edelweiss flower its face discloses,
In the morning of youth they found her,
    Dead, on a bed of roses!

Ah, Reality's beautiful picture, we cry!
    Though somewhat sad be the scene,
Gone, with youth's flushed cheek and star-lit eye,
    And beauty's brilliant gleam.

No troubles will that pure heart encumber,
    Behold, how tranquilly she reposes!
Ah, fair jewel thus gone to slumber,
    On a bed of Alpine roses!

In the morning of youth they found her,
    But know not her home nor her name,
But a breath of purity lurks round her,
    And shows her free from all blame.

Perhaps she died with a young love-dream,
   Yet fate oft sadness discloses,
So sleep, fair one, sleep calm and serene,
   On a bed of Alpine roses!

FANNY FERN.

BRAVE, struggling woman, noble work of God's creation,
  Reviewing the rough ground on which thou stood,
The trials of thy once lowly humble station,
   We say "She hath done what she could;"
While we face the world's oppressions fierce and stern,
Bright on memory's page be the name of Fanny Fern!

The howling tempests braved for thy children's sake
  Amid the dashing waves of want and strife,
And how vividly those sweet memories awake,
   As we view the pages of thy heroic life;
Prized lessons of womanly courage there we learn,
And treasure the efforts of the famed Fanny Fern.

Literary aspirants striving for pen-earned bread,
   Dwell o'er the many a by-meandering lane,
Thro' which, to reach the goal, thy weary feet did tread,
   And view with love, thy crispy name;
And while back and forth fortune's wheel may turn,
Strive to win a name as fair as Fanny Fern.

Still that *nom de plume* is not from justice's store,
   For, to the casual, unsearching eye,
Aside from thought's broad, expansive door,
   Its signification would seem dry;
But penetrating into the depths of thy mind's deep urn,
We cherish the modest signature of Fanny Fern.

Memory enshrines thee and hearts grow warmer,
   Warm, lost, familiar star, towards thee,
For we miss that sparkling little corner
   Of life's vast, literary sea;
But to the valued words we e'er shall fondly turn,
Nor e'er forget the name of patient Fanny Fern.

A MEMORY OF NEW YEAR'S EVE.

INSCRIBED TO M. L.

'Tis New Year's Eve, and with tear-filled eye,
I recall another from the long gone by,
   A New Year's Eve that thirty years have slid o'er,
   And blurred by the rough waves of care,
But now in the waning hours of 'seventy-four,
   Memory views through time's lurid air;
And is it weakness to plunge into realms of the Past,
To muse o'er my first joyful hour and the last?

Remorseless Time with his protean glass,
Has known many a scene like that, alas !
   Astrals were burning, the gilded corridors between,
     Wine was sparkling and music was loud,
   'Twas then that I heard my fond love dream,
     In the brilliant conservatory, away from the crowd,
His fervency tinged with the warmth of the sunny southern clime,
Yet his ardent love could not excel mine.

On such hair-like threads our destinies hinge,
That most trivial acts should make us cringe,
   For that same year had not neared its close,
     Ere in the height of mirth, with healthful breath,
   He sipped the poison, nor as the golden chalice rose
     Dreamed he drained the drugs of death,
One pulseless heart, one breathing, they closed within the grave,
And over them the orange and magnolia wave.
   CHICAGO, Dec. 31, 1874.

GIVE YOUR OLD CLOTHES AWAY.

   You wonder at *that*, and think it is wrong,
     Wait, and I'll explain what I say,
On what conditions it seems to be right,
     To give your old clothes away.

You, wealthy and blessed with abundant stores,
　Come in contact with those every day,
On whom you could confer untold good,
　By giving your old clothes away.

Then if *you* don't frequent the dry good's shops,
　Who'll purchase their contents so gay?
Surely not the poor class of people,
　To whom you should give old clothes away.

By giving merchants your custom, clothes to the needy,
　Buying a fresh suit for yourself, displeasing to none,
Behold how much at one time you'd do,
　Kill three birds with only *one* stone.

It teaches your daughters economy, you say,
　But it's a tendency toward miserly doing,
From which bad habits might eventually rise,
　Nor hardly the path for young feet's pursuing.

A story goes of one woman who economized,
　And planned sedulously, work upon her lap,
And when the day drew to a close,
　She'd made from out a *sheet*, a whole *night-cap*.

Yet economy, how highly we prize it,
　Economy of a kind that will pay,
But true economy on the whole, 'twould seem,
　Would it not? to give old clothes away!

TO MY MOTHER ON HER BIRTHDAY.

FROM " FORGET-ME-NOT."

MAY'ST thou to-day, dull care put away,
  And may happiness near thee hover,
May a bright ray near thee stay,
  On this, thy birthday, dear Mother.

And as o'er vanished years, thro' a mist of tears,
  Memory flies quick and fast,
Oh, dry thy tears, and all doubts and fears,
  Far from thee cast

Do not sigh for the years gone by,
  But rather thank our Heavenly Father,
Who from on high, with loving eye,
  Has spared and watched over thee, dear mother.

Now may He hear my prayer, and kindly spare
  Thee to see many a birthday more,—
When through with care, and this false world fair,
  Receive thee on that beautiful shore.

WHAT SHALL WE LEAVE ON MEMORY'S PAGE?

As we look back over the year that's almost past,
Year with clouds and sunshine overcast,
And record another year on Time's revolving stage,
The thought arises as we ponder o'er
The varied events memorizing 'Seventy-four,
What record would we leave on Memory's wide page?

Round us hope and ambition still survive.
And move toward the door of 'Seventy-five,
Not feeble and relaxing, but animated and undaunted,
And it were well, for without an aim in view,
Life would become dull and blue,
And this grovelling world be soon dis'chanted.

Something to win on Memory's sheet a claim,
That the world may not forget our name ;
But then, life's dewy promises are so transparent, thin,
That as we review aspirations of 'Seventy-four,
For past regrets we'd have amends in store !
And nobly strive for the guerdon we would win.

Then not mere wealth, or pomp, or fame,
Should be the nucleus of our aim,
But that some humble lip can have to say,

When our spirits have soared aloft,
" Her kind words have cheered me oft,"
Ah, brightest memory, to live, and live for aye.

CHICAGO, Dec. 20, 1874.

JOHNNIE THE BOOTBLACK.

JOHNNIE was an orphan, but he was honest and neat,
    And he had a head and a mind,
Though he blacked boots at the side of the street,
    Blacked them, and how they shined!

And days went by and six years passed,
    And Johnnie was clerk in a druggist's store,
He labeled the drugs and dealt them out,
    And blacked wayside boots no more!

And so faithful Johnnie labored and toiled,
    And another ten years glided away,
And journals praised, and tongues praised more,
    The skillful efforts of Dr. John Day.

And eight years more went into the past,
    · And Johnnie was traveling over the water,
When he met—and ever blessed the day—
    The Baron's beautiful daughter!

No happier couple e'er stood at St. Peter's altar—
Skeptic who laughs at the Bootblack and hoots,
Johnnie who won the Baron's beautiful daughter,
Once blacked the wayside boots!

THE LAST SABBATH OF THE YEAR.

ALL the months have sauntered by,
Bleak December's touch is here,
And its close now draweth nigh ;
There is an awe inspiring something near,
'Tis the last Sabbath of the year.

Let's turn our thoughts from the world away
Another year is numbered with the past,
On wingéd wings 't has fled away,
Our words, our acts it hath borne all too fast,
To the record that will always last.

Its Sabbaths so precious, all are o'er—
All! ah, there's one which seemeth doubly dear,
One remaining Sabbath more.
But soon e'en that will be no longer here,
For 'tis the last Sabbath of the year.

The snow is falling, falling without,
Within, perchanee, there is much to cheer,
But should there be one lurking doubt,
Let's go to him that calmeth every fear,
On this last Sabbath of the year.

Shall not coldness henceforth cease ?
With God, and man whom He hath placed here,
Let's determine to be at peace,
Let's free ourselves from every doubt and fear,
On this last Sabbath of the year.

THE BLIGHTED NAME.

REAL.

She was a beautiful girl with blonde-brown hair,
Hazel eyes and face so purely fair :
Her friends were counted by the score,
For kind fortune halted at her door;
But Misfortne's billows around her furled,—
She was alone and destitute in the world !
And one by one her friends were not,
Nor aught but depression was her lot;
Then woe to the day she met Claude Gaughlin,
A sheep's pure fleece, with a huge wolf in,
Her young love placed in his base protection,
Who cruelly gained her pure affection,

Lured her and stole her honor,
  Left her with the world's scorn upon her,
Henceforth upon her character a stain,
  A blight to mar for aye, her name :
Society's doors were closed, she soon descried,
  The vestibules of work denied,
Such the history of her they found to-day,
  Frozen to death on the cold railway.

A SPARK AT THE BOTTOM.

THE fire wouldn't go, and what to do, I didn't know,
  I was about turning away in despair,
When down through the dark, I discovered a spark,
  That I soon revived with care.

How well I felt, though, when a bright glow
  Rewarded my extra attention—
Tho' everything looks dark, we may discover a spark,
  That will be worthy of mention.

"GLANCES."

WHEN lips are so weak, that they can't speak,
  And emotions well up from the heart,
  The eyes unflinchingly take their part,
And how oft they look well what lips couldn't tell.

How many thrilling fancies, by some upward stealing glances
  May have been centered in the heart,
  From which 'twere agony to part—
Nothing more perchance, than a single passing glance.

This world is full of meetings, full of silent greetings,
  That lips fain would tell,
  And, perhaps, 'tis, yea, well,
For highly do we prize the lookéd greeting of the eyes.

Only a glance as we pass by, only a glance of the human eye,
  But quickly it reacheth the heart,
  Tho' we walk for aye and aye apart,
Though we meet no more, till we meet on that golden shore.

As, in that beauteous land, we in the same mansion stand
  I sometimes pause and think,
  As we from the golden chalice drink,
Will not uprise some silent meetings, may hap of some eye-
    glance greetings.

ONLY A BLACKSMITH'S SON.

" So kind, so noble, so generous in his way,
   Indeed I love him well,
But I'll be far from here at the close of another day."
   Soliloquized proud Adelle,
" And then I'll try to forget the heart I've won
'Twill never do, *only a blacksmith's son.*"

A maiden with silvery streaks in her hair,
   Looks o'er souveniers cherished long and well,—
Can it be she who was once so fair ?
   Ah, yes, 'tis the proud Adelle.
" How I have lived to rue the day,
I turned from his warm love away.

" Swiftly if not gayly the years have flown,
   But few that don't make some mistake,—
Then but remaineth, if I had known
   Which path was right to take,
I regret that I spurned the heart I won,
Tho' 'twas only the heart of a *blacksmith's son.*"

MY WOODLAND BOWER.

ASIDE from the hot sun's scorching ray,
Aside from the noisy world to-day,
   Where only my feathered pets are seen,
   Here 'mong the ferns and hedges green,
      I shut myself in :
Ah, 'tis my sanctum sanctorum this,
      And no malice, envy or sin.
Entereth my haven of bliss.

More beautiful than marble structure or tower,
'Tis Nature's own, my woodland bower,
   It harboreth no thought of strife,
   And here I find poetic life,—
      Put books and school away,
And bless this tranquil hour,
      Methinks that all around me lay,
Mysterious books in my woodland bower.

Nature hath formed my bough-twined seat
And a thousand books are at my feet,
   I behold one where e'er I look,
   For lo! the world's an open book;
School-books for the present, I'll lay aside,
   And study those that I have the power,
God shall be my teacher and guide,
   The schoolroom my woodland bower.

A RAY OF LIGHT.

E'EN when the clouds are thickest around,
E'en when grief is the most profound,
When there seems left not a star that is bright,
Still look to discern one ray of light.

ON THE DEATH OF A BRIDE.

DEATH, ever bringing sadness and gloom,
E'en dared to enter the bridal room,
  Death passing by stopped and entered there,
    And scanning the circle wide,
  Chose the loveliest and most fair,
    And she chanced to be a bride.
He feareth not to step upon any floor,
And boldly entereth the king's high door.

In her bridal wreath and robe of white,
We resigned her to the Lamb of light;
  No thorny paths had she ever trod,
    Her life was but a spring-time,
  Safe into the arms of her God,
    Did we our lost darling resign;
Few sins had she to be forgiven,
From a beautiful bride, to an angel in Heaven.

Oh, why should we shed one tear at all,
Or wish the loved one to recall?
    Life's voyage was just before, she stood on its verge,
      And rough its tide might have been,
    But she never knew its tumultuous surge,
      She died with her happy dream;
When we have wended thro' life's boist'rous tide,
May we again behold our " lost, resplendent bride."

JERUSHY AND JOE.

VERY fleshy was Jerushy Ophat, well what of that?
    Well, nothing, as you might say;
She fancied people very trim, so when she met Joe Slim,
    They fell in love straight-way.

Well, the girls made fun, but they didn't run,
    And how the boys did act,
Not when the girls whispered low, "Jerushy's engaged to Joe,"
    But when 'twas a decided fact.

" Oh, well," the boys would say, " it's too bad any way,
    Jerushy's plain-looking, I know,
But she's got a good heart, and I'm sure, for my part,
    I think she's too good for Joe."

With a smile, the girls would say, and turn scornfully away,
  "There, now, you're fibbing, you know,
The truth I'm willing to tell, Jerushy doesn't look well,
  And isn't good enough for Joe."

And so their hearts they'd discuss, with as much fuss,
  As tho' they'd been out of the common line ;
But Jerushy and Joe minded not a word of the gossip they heard,
  But calmly abided their time.

Ten years have passed away, since their wedding day,
  And happily they flit to and fro,
My friend, I know you have sense, then have fun at nobody's
    expense,
  Not even Jerushy and Joe.

ONLY A SILVER RING.

INCIDENTAL.

ONLY a silver ring, and yet methinks the angels sing,
  As I handle it o'er and o'er,
Ah, yes, it takes me back to that bright flooded track,
  Gone, to return no more.

And why tears should it bring, only a silver ring?
  "Very simple," I know you say,
But memory will linger, when 'twas put on my finger,
  The eighth of that far-off May.

In worldly effects, Ralph was poor, but no other wooer,
  E'er held a place in my heart,
Rich girl and poor lover, the tale of many another,
  We were forced to part.

But none other my heart could win, I remained true to him,
  And he crossed the ocean's tide,
Deceit's broad iron fetter, an intercepted letter,
  He won a foreign bride.

A heart generous and brave, he found a watery grave,
  In saving the life of a friend,
Thus for awhile we're parted, but I'll e'er prove true-hearted
  Till my sad life shall end.

Friends scarcely know me now, child of the sunny brow
  Grief such changes does bring,
Life is so bleak, and I am so lonely and weak,
  But I cherish the *silver ring*.

PURITY UNDEFILED.

We'd e'er lift an unfaltering hand to turn aside sin's cup,
Ever reach forth to lift a fallen sister up,
We'd e'en turn to those low down in vice and shame,
Nor yet would we despair of the vilest name.

We'd not pause to think that of those gone astray,
Such poor trifling hopes at the bottom lay;
But firmly reach forth a warm, reclaiming hand,
Despite the shallow ground on which we must stand;
Yet *joyfully* we turn to polish every pure name,
That it never *may wear* a blemish or stain,
For purity once blemished, *purity*, can not be styled,
And we'd strive to keep purity, *purity undefiled.*

FAREWELL.

Ah, the words wherewith to express the sensations
Of my overflowing heart come not to these trembling lips,
And Oh, I offer to you, my friends,
As a substitute for the welling emotions of this minute,
The equivalent of a volume wrapped in the solemn word,
        Farewell!

THE OLD HILL FARM.

INSCRIBED TO E. C.

'Tis old, and affords but a shelter from the storm,
But, oh, I love it—the house where I was born—
   'Tis the spot of childish sports and plays,
   Here standeth still the time-worn barn,
   And, oh, the cherished memories of by-gone days,
   That cluster round the old hill-farm:
Weary, dejected, and almost forlorn,
Still dear is the spot where I was born.

Here first my eyes beheld the light,
Here pattered my feet in childish delight,
   Here I watched the sun rise at early morn,
   Its last golden rays watched here,
   Oh, 'tis the spot where I was born,
   And here center associations dear.
It seemeth to me as a shield from harm,
And dear to me is the old hill-farm.

Each spot some sweet old story does tell,
I fain would not leave it 'mong strangers to dwell,
  Here wandered my father's departed feet,
  Here oft' my mother's stood,
  Familiar objects my eyes do greet,
  That carry me back to childhood,—
Here brothers and sisters have laughed and wept,
And friends who long in the grave have slept.

I'm a man now, past middle life,
Have fought in many a fierce field of strife,
  Have wished myself in " parts unknown,"
  Almost that my life would end,
  So rough the tempests have blown,
  And Fate, nothing but ills would send;
'Tis the only thing still holdeth a charm,
'Tis dear to me—the old hill-farm.

SHE ANSWERED NO.

INCIDENTAL.

ON *that scene*, just past the hour of twilight,
  So many years ago,
Surely the angels looked that night,
  And bade her answer no;
For, 'twas but a boyish heart he would have given,
Surely the angels looked down from Heaven.

It may have been a pleasant scene,
　While lips were preparing to meet,
But then, 'twas only a youthful dream,
　Tho' for the moment, 'twas very sweet,—
Perchance the lips may have even met,
And yet, 'twas not very hard to forget.

Surely the angels were good to bless
　That little twilight scene,
Suppose that she had answered yes,—
　Draw the curtain quick between :
The angels whispered that eve soft and low,
And firmly, but gently, she answered no.

At first it seemed a crushing dart,
　Something 'twould be hard to get over,
For she had won the yielding heart,
　Of her impulsive, but youthful lover.
That it was well, how plainly does time show,
The angels whispered that eve, and she answered no.

TWO HOMES.

Two pretty brides were Jennie and May,
   Vividly I recall them now,
Both stood at the altar the self-same day,—
   I hear the marriage vow.
May, with her dear sweet face,
   Was going to marry poor,
But Jennie with many a winning grace,
   Had a very wealthy wooer.

" Marry so poor," said Jennie, with a frown,
   I don't see how you can,
I'm going to have a house in town,
   " I never could marry a poor man;"
But Jennie got over her little pet,
   And both went up the aisle a bride,
And though my eyes for both were wet,
   I thought May has the better side.

That house is large, but it wants for care,
   And doesn't look neat within,
Showing at once that the dwellers there,
   Surely didn't rightly begin.
This one is smaller, but all is tasteful around,
   And there's a cheerful aspect of care,
Peace and happiness there abound,
   For love and contentment are there.

As I beheld them then with tearful eye,
Beheld each one a bride,
Though ten years have since gone by,
I think May has the better side.

I WAIT BESIDE THE RIVER.

A walk beside the Mohawk—an old woman who had met with the bitterest disappointments of life, sitting in a deep reverie, regardless of time—suggests the following:

I WAIT, and wait, and wait in vain,
For this poor head, so racked with pain,
Bids me not when to turn away,
And so for weary hours I stay,
'Till the evening mist sends a shiver,
I wait, wait beside the river.

Here I dream of life's few bright hours,
Recall the slight scattering of flowers,
That strewed so briefly life's pathway,
Then faded e'er the close of day;
To my heart comes pain's sharp quiver,
Still, I wait beside the river.

I gave ambition a firm grasp,
And love was warm within my clasp,
For a brief moment life was bright,
Then suddenly came the Night;
Ambition, cold deceiver, false, but fine,
Love, worshiper at Fashion's shrine.

Silver streaks the once brown hair,
Lines mar the cheek once fair,
And the eye of melting gray,
(As it was called in Fortune's day,
When I was flattered and admired,)
Weareth a look sleepy and tired.

As I watch Time keen whet his knife,
I ask myself, what is life?
And the answer comes softly back,
While a voyager on Life's rough track,
Trust Him, the bountiful Giver:
And thus I wait beside the river.

DELPHINE.

I PAUSE beside this flower-decked mound,
Recall her whom fifteen years had cycled round.
    Naught but gladness hadst thou seen,—
In this cold world with so rough a lot,
Is it wrong to envy thy resting spot?
    Oh, thrice happy Delphine!

Bright were the prospects thy path before,
Friends hadst thou by the score,
   And wealth flowed in an unbroken stream ;
But thou migh'st one day have lost them all,
And I see the wisdom of that early call,—
   A welcome Home, sweet Delphine!

Thou migh'st known Ambition's fond delusions,
And Love's gilded, but vain illusions,
   Have keenly felt and seen ;
Thou migh'st been left without a home,
Or e'en a friend to call thine own,—
   Better so, lovely Delphine!

Right out from a world of harm,
Fresh thy many a youthful charm,—
   Oh, had'st thou another score have seen,
This world with all its glitter and glare,
To the might not have been so fair,
   Happy art thou, lovely Delphine!

As, I pause beside this flower-decked mound,
Dear One, whom fifteen years had cycled round,
   Enviable is thy bed of green,—
No thorny pathway had'st thou trod,
Eere thou wert taken to the bosom of God,
   Lovely, early crowned Delphine!

MAY AND NOVEMBER.

INCIDENTAL.

ARM in arm they walked up the flower-strewn aisle,
Light hearts and lips wreathed with a happy smile,
Up to the altar, May and November, side by side,
And the village teacher becomes a Merchant's bride.

And the light gossip, conjuring if possible, the reason,
Why Lucy Randolph should gain " the catch" of the season.
Why mammas frowned and daughters repined?
Ah, his pockets with yellow gold were lined.

But while the sun shall rise and at night go down,
November upon May will not cease to frown;
Two months of such unlike, opposition weather,
May and November can never walk together.

November's cold restraint injures the flowery May,
And visibly she weareth from his side for aye and aye,—
Servants and carriage at her will and command,
She'd give them all to free her hand.

Freely resign her satins rich, and jewels rare,
To free her fettered mind from its burden of care,
And fain would exchange for her servant's part,
Could she give her hand where's gone her heart.

For that was left across the stormy waters,
Her penalty for vying with mothers and daughters,
The soft black eyes across the stormy deep,
Made sad havoc in her midnight sleep.

The light and sunken eyes on the pillow beside her own,
And the harsh gray locks from which all beauty'd flown,
And the hollow cheeks sunken at each side.
Illy contrasted with those across the tide.

But unknown to him love's sacred flame,
But for the unconscious breathing of a name,—
" Go," said he, " I'll see you across the stormy tide.
I see now you should have been another's bride."

" No, no, however much that step I may regret,
Thank God, I'm not so sinful yet,
Thine till death shall loose the chain,
If not God, man hath joined us twain."

Five years, and Death stopped at last,
In the mansion he so oft' had passed :
The busy brain and active hand were stilled,
To her was his princely fortune willed.

Three years since reverently she closed his eyes,
And once more she yearned for Italy's sunny skies;
And so she crossed again the mighty deep,
And climbed again Tivoili's romantic steep.

Once more in Nature's works she took delight,
Found charms in Venice's golden light,
And finding strength and spirit again her own,
She went where *they* once had been—to Rome.

A lovely morn, early in the bright Italian May,
When a party mostly young, and of spirits gay,
Set forth to see St. Mona's mystic Convent gloom,
And explore the mysteries of ancient Rome.

Who shall deny the Providence manifest in all?
The ramblers paused beside a grand old waterfall,
And sweet Lucy recalling the mysterious Sybil's fane,
Pondered her words: "Thou wilt be happy again."

But while they gazed on the scene by Nature painted,
A sudden scream, and Lucy'd fainted:
Round the evening shadows began to steal,
As they bore her into the Hotel de Ville.

Ah, 'twas no mere idle whim or fancy,
Her preserver was Raphael De Lancy;
He knew not that she heired a large estate,
Nor she, that he had rank and honor great.

And tho' for matronly grace she'd resigned her girlish smile,
A happier bride ne'er glided up St. Peter's aisle;
And when again she crossed the Atlantic's tide,
The dearest one of earth was at her side.

CHRISTMAS EVE.

AH, yes, another year with its rapid flight,
    With its promised pleasures that deceive,
Another year with all its changes, great or slight,
    Brings us to Christmas eve.

My mind is wandering far away,—
    May I not my dear Father grieve,
To my mind there rushes a brighter day,
    Revived by Christmas eve.

My mind is flighty, but my heart is true,
    Dear Father, I'll look to thee,
For thou wilt kindly lead me through,
    And guide me o'er Life's treacherous sea.
FRIDAY EVE., Dec. 24, 1874.

WAITING AT THE WINDOW.

SONG.

WAITING at the window, waiting at the window for thee,
The footstep that so oft I've heard,
    I'm waiting now to hear,
Its echo like the song of a bird,
    Is ringing in my ear :
Thy footstep shall I hear, and thy face shall I see,
Waiting at the window, waiting at the window for thee?

Waiting at the window, waiting at the window for thee,
Waiting, though 'tis early in the morn,
   And the clouds are dark and gray,
Oh, will thy well-known form
    Pass my window to-day?
Thy footstep shall I hear, and thy face shall I see,
Waiting at the window, waiting at the window for thee?

'Waiting at the window, waiting at the window for thee,
Though the clouds are dark without,
   Our Father knoweth best:
And he can clear the heart from doubt,
    And faith in Him can test,
Thy footstep I shall hear, and thy face I shall see,
Waiting at the window, waiting at the window for thee

Waiting at the window, waiting at the window for thee
Every cloud is fast disappearing,
   And the sun begins to shine,
Every doubt in my mind is clearing,
    Thy will, oh, God, be mine:
Thy footstep I shall hear, and thy face I shall see,
Waiting at the window, waiting at the window for thee.

Waiting at the window, waiting at the window for thee,
It comes! and what music it brings,
   The welcome sound I hear,
And my Guardian Angel sings,
    As it reaches my ear.
For thy footstep I hear, and thy face I see,
Waiting at the window, waiting at the window for thee.

Waiting at the window, waiting at the window for thee,
Now every cloud has gone from above.
    And the sun is shining bright,
And well I know that God is love,
    And doeth all things right.
Thy footstep I hear, and thy face I see,
Waiting at the window, waiting at the window for thee.

THE MORNING KISS.

SUGGESTED BY A PICTURE.

AH! I see the little curly head, just peeping from out its bed,
    And the next thing is a kiss.
    What a happy moment this!
It fills my cup of joy, the kiss of my darling baby boy!

I fear too bright my sun does shine, and while his lips meet
    mine,
    There cometh a feeling of sadness,
    While my heart is full of gladness,—
What a blank world this, without that morning kiss!

With his little mite of song, he creepeth lovingly along,
    Closes his star-like eyes,
    Slightly on his knees does rise,
Not a word does speak, while he leaves a kiss upon my cheek.

Little pet only three years old, but his wealth of love is untold,
   And I count it supreme bliss,
   To feel his soft morning kiss;
But I must set no great store, lest my cup full of joy run o'er.

SUNLIGHT IN THE EAST.

Many a day the ceaseless patter and dull trickle of rain,
   Have cast a cloud o'er this charming section,
Low down in the valley and up on the plain,
   Leaving a somber hue in every direction.
Here to quaff the beauties that environ the sea shore,
But no ray of sunlight have we seen here before,
But the clouds have dispersed, and the sun has come forth,
   O'er the gorgeous scene our eyes we will feast,
For, oh, how deeply do we prize the worth,
   Of the first sunlight we've seen in the East.
KINGSBURY, MASS., Aug., 1873.

THE YOUNG MAN'S FAREWELL TO HOME.

HOME of my childhood, home of my youth, I leave thee now,
   Home of Memory's sweetest scenes,
   Home of my youthful dreams!
Manlier will have grown this still puerile brow,
   Ere again I behold these evergreens;

But now I must close the old familiar gate,
And hasten, why should I longer wait?
My frail bark is just launching on life's great sea,
And shall it in the future waft joy or grief to me?

Father mother, brother, sister, I leave you all behind,
    Forth into the world alone I go,
    Many temptations I may know,
I shall miss those words so mild, so calm and kind,
    That e'er in gentle accents flow:
Yes, I leave you to sail out on life's stormy tide,
I leave you, dear ones, asking Divine power to guide—
To guide and waft my timerous, shallow bark,
Which must encounter clouds, fearful oftimes, and dark.

One lingering look, which, perchance, may be the last,
    Home of my childhood and youth,
    Home of sweet lessons—devotion and truth:
Ah, merry days, and how fleetly ye have passed!
    But why vain regrets, forsooth?
Dear ones, who've shared with me each joy and sigh,
Father, mother, brother, sister, all good-bye!
Time hastens, I must break the magic spell,
Home of my affection, fare thee well!

THE YOUNG MAN'S RETURN TO HOME.

YEARS have run into a channel numbered four,
    Since I left thee, belovéd home,
    It seems that I'd even older grown,
So many miles of experience have I passed o'er,
    And been by such fierce winds blown :
Old home welcome the wanderer as he come,
Room, too, and welcome for another one,
A welcome warmer and more dear,
For her who comes a stranger here.

Home that I left—there's the old familiar gate—
    Ah, Memory, hush ! be still !
    Why hint against my will,
That 'twas a rendezvous for me and Kate ?
    There's no niche but love now fill,
And yet, in a sweet, sad, long-buried dream,
There's a little grave o'ergrown with green,
If she had lived—but all is for the best,
Peace to the little form the sod thus early pressed.

There's the barn, the orchard, spot of childish days,
    Four years have touched thee lightly,
    For the sun but shines more brightly,
Upon thee now, than e'en in former days,
    Each scene is sure as fair and sightly,—

Ah, you hasten to welcome me, my father, mother,
Enlarge that welcome then to enfold another,
Sister, mother—all—a better one is waiting now,
Place the warmest kiss upon *her* brow.

A PICTURE OF MEMORY.

A SPACIOUS storehouse filled with many a choice thing,
    The sweetest and the best,
I've flowers that bloom and birds that sing,
    And much that gives me rest.
Many a picture gilded and rare,
    Hangs on Memory's wall,
But of all the pictures hung with care,
    One seemeth better than all.
I've pictures of forests dim and gray,
    And pieces of toys broken,
And visions of gardens bright and gay,
    And many a childish token;
A Chromo of happy childhood's hours,
    Has a lovely perfumed frame,
And bunches of faded myrtle and flowers,
    Each labeled with a name;
And there's a face with eyes of black,
    Once my teacher and guide,
When first o'er the stormy track,
    My feet commenced to slide,—

Then there's a cottage by sweet briar kissed,
  And pansies before the door,
Then a dim, uncertain mist,
  The cottage is no more.
Then there are schools loved and dear,
  The Cottage and Houghton Sem,
And an old red building in the rear,
  That was hung before them,—
Sweet faces that did my mind direct;
  And two other schools are there,
Only called by the name Select,
  And a familiar look they wear.
I've pictures, too, of a later date,
  Scarcely soiled by time,
I've pictures small, and pictures great,
  Whose originals once were mine.
But of all the pictures hung with care,
  Hung on Memory's wall,
There's one seems more sad and fair,
  That seemeth best of all.
A day in the month of October,
  A little hand clasped in mine,
A face by turns merry and sober,
  Playing strawberry time ;
A playhouse by the moss-covered well,
  'Neath the Sycamore branches nigh,
Our only dish a scraped out cocoanut shell,
  The people, my cousin Willie and I;
And of all the pictures on Memory's wall,
  Pictures hung with care,

I prize that one above them all,
 It looketh sad but fair.
Near where the Sycamore ʋranches wave,
 Softly, calmly and stilly,
I've hung the picture of a little grave,
 The grave of cousin Wlllie.
Of those hours so joyful and gay,
 When last I played with him,
Of that far off, gladsome day,
 I've only a picture, and that is dim;
But of all the chromos on Memory's wall,
 Though it is faded and gray,
To me, it seemeth best of all,
 The picture of *that* day.

HAPPY NEW YEAR, DEAR MAMMA!

THE Old Year has gone, mamma, we've stepped thro' the protean
 door,
To welcome the successor of Eighteen-seventy-four:
 Four seasons more have rolled away,
 They've bro't sorrow in multifarious forms,
 Some sunshine sprinkled along the way,
 To appease life's beating storms;
But the year with its wondrous vicissitudes is o'er,
We've said good-bye to 'Seventy-four:
 And as we this day have lived to see,
 A happy New Year, mamma—
 A happy New Year let me wish to thee!

Misfortunes have come, yet would I strive,
To smile on the ushering day, of 'Seventy-five ;
    Truly, it is in the year that is past,
      We've met the reverses of !ife,
    Which e'en now dark clouds overcast,
      And fiercest·of tempests are rife ;
Still we'd smile on the New Year, dear mother,
Grateful we're spared to behold another ;
    And amid the hurricanes that threaten life's sea,
      I'll turn, and a happy New Year mamma—
    A happy New Year I'll wish to thee !

    CHICAGO, Jan. 1., 1875.

BUSY THE HAND TO STILL THE HEART.

WHEN the world looks dark, and the heart beats swift,
    O'ercome with many a piercing dart,
Then bid patience her magic wand up-lift,
    And busy the hand to still the heart.

When the heart is bubbling over with sorrow,
    And throbs of anguish thro' each nerve start,
Questioning Hope in vain for a bright to-morrow,
    Then busy the hand to still the heart.

When on the edge of despair you sit,
    From steadfast Faith apart,
When the lamp of Courage's no longer lit,
    Busy the hand to still the heart.

When the roughest storms that life may know,
Cause trembling and fear to start,
When tempests of strife all hurriedly blow,
Busy the hand to still the heart.

SLEEP, DEAR MOTHER.

On discovering the loss of MSS., and canvassing list and other property after the July fire.

GENTLY, dear Mother, gently sleep,
Knowing not the tumults deep,
That in thy darling's breast are pounding;
Gently, dear Mother, gently sleep,
For the angels a vigil keep,
O'er the heart's pulsing and bounding.

Gently, dear Mother, gently sleep,
For 'twould but cause thee to weep,
To know of the wild surging and throbbing;
Gently, dear Mother, gently sleep,
For angels a vigil keep,
While anguish of sweet rest is robbing.

Gently, Dear Mother, gently sleep,
For God watcheth his sheep,
E'en while the elements are raging;
Gently, dear Mother, gently sleep,
For the angels a vigil keep,
While the tempest each tho't is engaging.

Gently, dear Mother, gently sleep,
For my cares shall not sweep
O'er thy peaceful pillow a pain;
Gently, dear Mother, gently sleep,
For the angels a vigil keep,
O'er the heart s garden where frost work is lain.

Gently, dear Mother, gently sleep,
For quietness may creep,
O'er my disturbed and restless pillow;
Gently, dear Mother, gently sleep,
For angels a vigil keep,
To quiet, if best, each foaming billow.

THE UNKNOWN TOMB.

VAST Monument! that with sublimity doth stand,
To memorize the fallen heroes of our land!
Glorious Monument, proud and grand!
By thy cold, unpitying side we pause and weep,
For those who once made happy many a home,
Who now beneath this art-carved marble sleep,
The tomb engraved "unknown;"
And in fancy we hear the drums, behold the sword and shi
And the dark scenes of a Southern battle-field!

Over these unknown ones we shed a tribute tear,
Over the fallen heroes who now are sleeping here,
Who fell undaunted, and without fear;

Here we would twine a memorial wreath o'er their brow,
    Though no record bear their personal fame,
Here we would not forget them now,
    Tho' nativity be unknown, alike unknown their name,
Know that they a brave heroic life did yield,
Recall to mind that blood-strewn battle-field!

And now as this hallowed spot we turn to leave,
Let fond memory, and affection weave
    A garland o'er which time may breathe;
Yet never pale and dim with sighs or tears,
    A garland that but brighter grows,
As time forms a wide abyss of. years,
    Such a garland for these fallen heroes,
Whom thou unknown tomb doth shield,
Unknown ones of a Southern battle-field!
And may our successors when high Time's pyramid doth loom
Muse sometimes beside the " Unknown Tomb."

WASHINGTON, D. C., Dec. 20, 1873.

EXPECT THE WORST AND HOPE FOR THE BEST.

IN this world where waves of trouble ever are rolling,
    And discouragement is ofttimes a guest,
If, perchance, there's a fond hope with its gentle consoling,
    Expect the worst and *hope* for the best.

There's a full cup of joy, perhaps, that's almost your own,
　And *may* soon in your expectant clasp rest,
Yet many such ones rude winds have blown,
　Then *expect* the worst and *hope* for the best.

Where life were witness to volumes of incoming sorrow,
　And for the faint possibility of a forthcoming joy thirst,
Blight not the hope, nor undue misgivings borrow,
　Nor *less hope* for the best, but be *prepared* for the wors..

The best needs no precedent its arrival to announce.
　'Twill be joyfully welcomed as animation will attest,
But Oh, lest its rival swoop down with deft, sudden pounce,
　Calmly *expect* the worst, still *hope* for the best.

An emergency armor were safe fortified by an alternative plan,
　For there's many an *if* in this field of contest,
And much that is promising may prove but a sham,
　Then *expect* the worst and *hope* for the best.

DEAD.

ANOTHER bud hath withered now
　Only six months o'er its little head,
Yet cold and still the snowy brow,
　The infant boy is dead.

In that little crib now set aside,
　May rest other brows of snow,
And who'll think ot the baby that died—
　That died so long ago?

Tho' there in infant beauty rest,
　The form of many another,
Tho'ts of the lost will haunt the breast
　Of that fond and loving mother.

" Finis" is once more engraved
　On time's hoary page,
And we know that he is saved,
　Sweet one of beauty's age.

The angels on their glorious throne,
　His pearly brow are kissing,
And they will bless the vacant home,
　Where his little form is missing.

BENEATH WHITE TIES.

INCIDENTAL.

'Twas a marble mansion, tall and stately **grand,**
　Fortune smiled benignly on their store,
And many was the outstretched hand,
　Bore a tribute from their door:

On the wings of joy, Charity was bade to perch,
    As Time fulfilled its marked rotation,
The wayside beggar, the College, and the Church,   ·
    Shared in their magnificent donation ;
But alas, how fleeting the possessions of frail human life !
The heart of Prosperity rent by one stroke of Fate's quick acrid
    knife !

Why the ins and outs, and whys and wherefores here repeat ?
    A weary trudge the acme of prosperity to reach,
Only *one* step from the affluent broker to a beggar in the street,
    So doth delusive Fortune teach !
A sinking ship on a rough, raging tide,—
    A burning and crashing of the marble block,
A widow with five children at her side,
    Sits in the cradle where want and sorrow rock !
So slender the thread on which hangs joy or woe,
That in either, it may break before we know.

She had succored others, the world would not forget her,
    The *world* was not prone perchance to remember ;
While whispered words, winks and nods *would* occur,
    In the stone edifice of which she was a member ;
But there is a Temple not reared by mortal hand,
    On which, we our hopes may build :
A loftier temple that will always stand
    With fair heart treasures filled.
Blest tho't, said she, there's still One Divine Spirit of the skies !
Who scanneth all, nor is deceived by wearing of white ties.

A SHINING TEMPLE.

AH, there's a shining Temple on a Hill,
  And its lights illume for aye,
And it never bringeth woe nor ill,
  To those that pass that way.

A brighter Temple than e'er was built by hand,
  It containeth jewels rich and rare,
Brilliant gems from all the lands
  Are closely clustered there.

The gems of Faith, Hope and Contentment,
  Charity and all of her allies.
And Hatred, Envy or Resentment,
  Ne'er in its precincts lies.

On the Hill of Humility, o'er the rill of Confession,
  Standeth Religion's Temple so bright,
Supported forever by gentle Discretion,
  Surely, 'tis a Temple of light.

But who in this beautiful Temple dwell?
  Not all who the title claim,
But *one day* 'twill be known full well,
  For there's a Record bears each name.

"COLLEGE HILL."

In a fair Eastern valley known as the "Oriskany,"
  The town's name I need not mention;
Useless to crook it into feeble poesy,
  For *some* will give it their attention.
Those who've climb'd that slope in search of knowledge
  Must vividly, methinks, remember still
The name of town—alike the name of College
  Which proudly stands upon this hill.

The town itself has much for Memory's store,
  Nor with care nor diligence need she search,—
Three noted Temples of Learning, others a full score,
  That Temple of Worship known as the "Stone Church."
The Park just opposite—but you'll know where—
  The Burnt District (they talked of building—hope they **will)**
But all these would court Oblivion's air,
  While Memory sticks by "College Hill."

Oh, dear! why is it thus? I'm sure I was no favorite there:
  Young in years, plain in looks, and void of wealth,
I couldn't hope (and had no wish, in fact,) to share
  Flirtations, joys gained by studied stealth.
Ah, kind teachers! beware an unpretending book-worm chit,
  Watch for deep water tho' it may run still;
Such an one may have just enough of wit,
  To aid the boarder's *billet-doux* to "College Hill."

And my favorites (the girls I mean, of course,)
　　Oh! how faithfully I worked for them!
Perhaps I ought to feel sorrow and remorse
　　For *such* an act in that belovéd Sem.
But then, how can I feel even a blush of shame,
　　When their sweet smiles haunt me still?
I guess that they'll remember, without a scribbled name,
　　The communication channel 'tween them and " College Hill."

French and Grecian History, ah, yes! I loved them well,
　　But before them float these words upon my ear:
Before the heroes of Virgil and Fasquelle—
　　Those words—shall I record them here?
Words as some message had by me been wended,
　　Sweet words. that haunt me still:
" Oh, I'm so much obliged! you're just splendid! "
　　Bright reminescence of yonder " College Hill! "

Though many a cosy haunt and favorite scene
　　Rises to Memory's pellucid sight,
There's many a fair and beauteous dream,
　　Faded in dim Oblivion's night;
But amid those scenes that have gradually paled away,
　　And 'mid those that are remaining still,
There's one that stands conspicuous to-day,
　　And that is " College Hill."

" ONE LOVING HEART."

TO MAMMA.

THE world and its petty allurements thick around
   Transient hopes and joys may fling,
Bid happiness for awhile with us abound,
   Yet how fleet is all the joy they bring.
In undying rays of Love and Peace they do not bask,
   And how soon their gilded rays depart!
Oh, to prize *them* were a sorry task
   Beside one loving heart.

The poet may wear a laurel wreath,
   Some wealth's baubles may enfold;
And still their gilded show beneath
   May lie sorrow and woe untold:
Oh, who could ever wish to wear
   Symbols that no true peace impart;
What can ever be as pure and fair
   As one loving heart!

Precious stones from Australian mines,
   Treasures from the distant sea,—
Keep them! yes, a thousand times,
   And leave one loving heart for me!
Leave the monarch his palace, and queen her throne,
   Little joy to me could they impart;
Much rather would I happily own
   One loving heart.

ON THE PINNACLE.

On the pinnacle of—may we call it destruction?
  Led thither by o'erwhelming waves of despair,
Viewing the pros of its enticing seduction,—
  And did you ever stand there?
Satan close eyeing distress lights on a deep one,
  And nods at allurements over the hill;
You may hint that you'll go, 'tis *your* risk you run—
  The world says, go if you will

Halting between two evils—but no, one evil,
  For the other is golden-plumed Right,
She's away from that hill, and away from the devil,
  Though dark are the shadows as night.
Pure death or dark life—then the former, we cry!
  Peace be to that heart spotless and still,
And the cold world with its cynical eye,
  Remember, says go if you will.

Somebody, sometime, perchance in unborn ages,
  Somewhere, in a native or foreign place,
May chance to look on these simple pages,
  While cold and starvation stare them in face;
Then let one whose sympathy is deep and untold,
  Conjure you to turn from that hill,
Stand firmly in the portals of Right's castle fold
  For the world says, go if you will.

'Tis not the world's loss or gain, but 'tis yours;
 Then keep your conscience and spotless name
For a lost life the world no grief endures,
 Nor knows a blush or a tinge of shame.
Consider you've a fortune at your hand,
 While you avoid that Satanic hill;
Face death itself, but pure and upright stand,
 For the world says, go if you will.

TO M. J. M.,

ON HER SIXTH BIRTHDAY.

Six times the years have circled round,
 And touched thy golden hair;
Six times thou hast heard the sound,
 Of Spring birds in the air;
Six times Winter's breath has fanned
 Thy brow of ivory white;
Six times thy little hands have planned
 Summer's nosegays bright.
Six times the crimson Autumn bud
 Thy rosy cheek hath shamed,
And her rich and beauteous flood,
 'Fore thy violet eyes hath reigned.
And thou standest 'mid the gay,
 Minus one grief or tear,
To welcome thy glad birthday,
 And enter thy seventh year.

We wish thee joy, dear little one,
  As we crown thy wavy hair,
May thy life, so beautifully begun,
  Ne'er be less bright and fair.

CLOSING LINES.

To you who to these pages have lent your kind attention,
My thanks I'd speak, my gratitude would mention;
Let me wish that many a blessing, many an offering true,
Fate behind her curtain may have in store for you.
May you have found a trifling thought upon some page,
That you'll keep for aye on life's great stage:
May some cheerful element for each one lurk
Within the out-stretched arms of modest " Patchwork."
A word—a thought—trifling though perchance it be,
May comfort 'mid the billows of Life's tempestuous sea;
Oh! let not the little lustre of my simple rhymes be marred,
Or judged by some standard author, or by some ancient bard;
You've read their works perhaps a dozen times or more,
Look kindly on one just stepping to the literary floor;
Should it seem unpolished in Tennyson's society,
You surely will admit that the spice of life's *variety*;
And its flaws and failings, please to pass them o'er,
And treasure but the best in Memory's vast store:
She says in plaintive voice: " Accept my wayward verse;
Accept it kindly—' for better or for worse;'"

And one day on a griefless shore in a golden street,
May the readers and author of " Patchwork " meet;
There 'mid countless brows, ne'er frowning but pleasant ·
Thus I bid you all good-bye for the present.

INDEX.

www.ingramcontent.com/pod-product-compliance
Lightning Source LLC
Chambersburg PA
CBHW020849270326
41928CB00006B/611